D0064640

Joyce Carol Oates
Novels of the Middle Years

Twayne's United States Authors Series

Warren French, Editor
University College of Swansea, Wales

TUSAS 597

JOYCE CAROL OATES
Photograph © Jerry Bauer

Joyce Carol Oates
Novels of the Middle Years

Joanne V. Creighton

Wesleyan University

Twayne Publishers • New York
Maxwell Macmillan Canada • Toronto
Maxwell Macmillan International • New York Oxford Singapore Sydney

Joyce Carol Oates: Novels of the Middle Years
Joanne V. Creighton

Twayne Publishers   Maxwell Macmillan Canada, Inc.
Macmillan Publishing Company   1200 Eglinton Avenue East
866 Third Avenue   Suite 200
New York, New York 10022   Don Mills, Ontario M3C 3N1

Macmillan Publishing Company is part of the Maxwell Communication Group
of Companies.

Library of Congress Cataloging-in-Publication Data

Creighton, Joanne V., 1942-
    V. Creighton.
    Joyce Carol Oates : novels of the middle years / Joanne
        p.   cm. — (Twayne's United States authors series ; TUAS 597)
    Includes bibliographical references and index.
    ISBN 0-8057-7647-8
    1. Oates, Joyce Carol, 1938-   —Criticism and interpretation.
I. Title.   II. Series.
PS3565.A8Z615   1992
813'54—dc20   91-42035
                                                        CIP

The paper used in this publication meets the minimum requirements
of American National Standard for Information Sciences—Permanence
of Paper for Printed Library Materials. ANSI Z3948-1984. ∞™

10 9 8 7 6 5 4 3 2 1

Printed in the United States of America

To my sister, Judy

Contents

Preface

This book is a companion to my earlier volume in this series, *Joyce Carol Oates*, first published in 1979. The critical scope of that book included Oates's short story collections and novels published from 1963 through 1976. This volume picks up where the earlier left off, covering the period 1977–90 but restricting its focus, for the most part, to the 15 novels written during this time. As in the first volume, I look carefully at Oates's essays, especially the more recent ones, which are important critical statements in their own right and provide revealing insights into her fiction. While I fill out a bit more the sketchy biographical portrait I drew in the first volume, my primary focus remains the Joyce Carol Oates who is a voice in her writing—both fictional and nonfictional—rather than on the living, breathing person, Joyce Smith. The problematic relationship between her two selves fascinates the author: indeed, the problematic nature of the self continues to be a central subject of her oeuvre.

I am much more convinced than I was 12 years ago that Joyce Carol Oates has now earned a secure place as one of our truly significant American writers. To be sure, she is a phenomenon—a writer of extraordinary productivity who had by 1985 generated over 1,000 published items, according to a 1986 bibliography. It is hard to keep count: as of this writing she has published 23 novels (three pseudonymously) and at least 15 short-story collections, 10 volumes of poetry, 6 edited volumes, 3 plays, and literally hundreds of reviews, scholarly articles, occasional essays, journalistic pieces, and interviews. And no abatement in her writing is evident: in fact, she is rumored to have a file drawer full of completed manuscripts awaiting publication.

But productivity alone does not make Joyce Carol Oates significant; rather, the range, depth, and variety of her work and the cogency of her thought earn her distinction. Drawing her inspiration from personal and cultural contexts as well as from literary and intellectual sources, she scrutinizes, in work after work, the nature of American character, culture, and literary tradition. She is an experimental writer who, as John Barth has commented, "writes all over the aesthetical map."[1] She dares to tackle a variety of subjects and to employ a range of techniques, and in so doing she dares to risk failure. While her success is uneven, she has received far worse press than she deserves. Much of her work is genuinely distinguished; taken as a totality, it is an incredibly rich, impressive testament to her lively intellect and creative genius. It is a substantial body of work deserving more recognition and critical attention than it is usually accorded.

While many people have read a story or a novel or two by Oates, very few readers invest the time that would be needed to keep up with her prodigious output, to see each work in the context of her unfolding canon. Even a sympathetic and conscientious reader like myself (who has undertaken to write two books on the author) still has a great deal of difficulty in keeping up. I confess that I find it impossible to read all that Oates has written, much less all that she has read; elusive, she sprints buoyantly ahead of any attempt to assess her achievement.

No ready labels, no firm critical contexts have been established to place Joyce Carol Oates; her variegated work makes her highly resistant to categorization. Still, the role of a critic is to comment, and that I do in this volume. Knowing that I am risking overstatement and oversimplification, I have yet attempted to stake out a critical trail for others to follow, or to abandon, through the dense and uncharted terrain of Oates's work. Given the nature and purpose of this critical introduction, my observations are necessarily speculative and broadly stroked. In short, I argue throughout this volume that in valuing the resilient kernel of selfhood and the tenacious will to endure, prevail, and transcend limitations, Oates remains deeply, if somewhat ironically, subscribed to the traditions of American romanticism.

Chapter 1 examines the personal and conceptual context of Oates's fiction. Chapter 2 looks at *Son of the Morning* (1978), *Unholy Loves* (1979), *Cybele* (1979), and *Angel of Light* (1981)—novels that are part of Oates's multivolume study of representative professional subcultures within American society. Though widely varying in perspective, tone, and method, these novels portray "love-obsessed" characters. Theirs are romantic quests, fraught with pitfalls and delusions and intermixed with the baser emotions, and the authorial perspective is sometimes ironic and satiric. Yet the aspiring spirit is not always portrayed as foolish; sometimes it finds redemption through "holy" or "unholy" love.

Chapter 3 focuses on the most ambitious and experimental of Oates's fiction, her portraits of America "as viewed through the prismatic lens of its most popular genres"[2]—*Bellefleur* (1980), *A Bloodsmoor Romance* (1984), and *Mysteries of Winterthurn* (1984). Here is Oates at the height of her creative powers, playfully exploiting the intertextual possibilities of her intellectual and literary inheritance. Reimaginings of popular American nineteenth-century genres, these works are fabulations that ironically call attention to their own artifice. Although playful, these novels, like all her work, are serious studies of American character, American society, and the American dream. For one thing, to reenvision American culture and history through its popular genres is to see more clearly their stridently patriarchal foundations and their pervasive misogyny.

In her subsequent works of realistic fiction—*Solstice* (1985), *Marya: A Life* (1986), and *You Must Remember This* (1987), considered in chapter 4—Oates focuses on warring dualities within the female psyche itself. Among other things, these works are studies of the dialectics of female friendship, selfhood, and creativity. In both her essays and her fiction, the later Joyce Carol Oates is increasingly feminist in perspective, exploring her heritage as a woman and as a woman writer.

Curiously coupled with this sharpened focus on female identity is Oates's recent writing on an exclusively masculine sport, boxing. Boxing, for a woman, says Oates, is a study of "the other"—the male. But boxing is also yet another arena in which to examine the dialectics of emotion and will, "the quintessential . . . struggle, masculine or otherwise, against not only other people but one's own divided self."[3] I look at Oates's nonfiction book *On Boxing* (1987) in chapter 5, along with three novels she published under the pseudonym Rosamond Smith: *Lives of the Twins* (1987), *Soul/Mate* (1989), and *Nemesis* (1990). These novels too, in both theme and method, are studies of "the other"; they are conspicuous redefinitions of the writerly self.

In *American Appetites* (1989) and *Because It Is Bitter, and Because It Is My Heart* (1990), which I look at in chapter 6, Oates returns to the characteristic themes and situations of the main body of her fiction. In both novels the American dream is fractured by an unintentional killing; in both, violence is an upwelling of tension, breaking through the civil games of society and the conscious control of character; in both, appetites of the soul remain unfulfilled. In *Because It Is Bitter* Oates casts her portrayal of the self and "the other" in a racial context, adding a potent new dimension to her study of American character and society.

In the concluding chapter I examine the contexts and contradictions of Oates's critical reception. She was called in one early review the "dark lady of American letters."[4] That label is not at all right. She has tremendous respect for the dark side of human experience, for the mysterious depths of the unconscious, and for the primitive brutality at the core of physical existence. Yet Joyce Carol Oates's vision is not dark. She is in fact optimistic about the possibilities of human resilience and transcendence of a distinctly American variety. She recognizes the deep drives within the human psyche,

and especially within the artist, to break through narrow and rigid definitions of selfhood: to balance the almost dialectic dualities of consciousness
and unconsciousness, male and female, public and private, inner and outer,
self and other, life and fiction; to push against the outer parameters of one's
being.

One of the pleasures of writing about a living author is that she can write
back, engage in dialogue. I would like to thank Joyce Carol Oates, who
kindly and thoughtfully read and critiqued an earlier draft of this manu-
script, and whose commentary has helped immeasurably to sharpen my
reading of her work. Of course, I alone am responsible for the critical views
put forward in this study. Of my emphasis on her postmodern romanticism,
Oates comments:

I don't disagree about the theme of "romanticism"—I've always believed that all
writers, and no doubt all artists, are romantics of a kind, since to attempt to create
something out of nothing, often in the face of the world's indifference or outright
hostility, is certainly a romantic and idealistic act. Beyond that, or in a kind of interior dialogue with that, there are of course gradations of self-scrutiny; counter-
romantic impulses.[5]

This study, then, looks at the considerable "something out of nothing" that
Joyce Carol Oates evokes and scrutinizes in her impressive oeuvre.

I thank my husband, Tom, and my son, Will, for their tolerance and for-
bearance, and "all the good people I've left behind" and remember fondly at
the University of North Carolina at Greensboro for their support and en-
couragement of this project.

Chronology

1938   Born June 16, daughter of Caroline and Frederick Oates, eldest of three children. Grew up in the countryside of Erie County outside Lockport, New York, on maternal grandparents' farm.

1956–1960   Attended Syracuse University on New York State Regents scholarship. Phi Beta Kappa; class valedictorian; earned B.A. in English, minor in philosophy.

1959   Cowinner, first prize, *Mademoiselle* College Fiction Contest for "In the Old World."

1960–1961   Attended University of Wisconsin, Madison, on fellowship; 1961, met and married Raymond Joseph Smith; earned M.A. in English.

1961–1962   Lived in Beaumont, Texas; started work on Ph.D. at Rice University, Houston.

1962–1967   Taught English at University of Detroit.

1963   *By the North Gate* (stories).

1964   *With Shuddering Fall* (novel).

1965   "The Sweet Enemy" (play) premiered at Actor's Playhouse, New York City.

1966   *Upon the Sweeping Flood* (stories); National Endowment for the Humanities Grant.

1967–1968   Guggenheim Fellowship.

1967   Joined Department of English, University of Windsor, Windsor, Ontario; *A Garden of Earthly Delights* (novel); first prize, O. Henry Prize Awards, for "In the Region of Ice."

1968   *Expensive People* (novel); *Women in Love* (poems); Richard and Hilda Rosenthal Foundation Award of the National Institute of Arts and Letters for *A Garden of Earthly Delights;* National Endowment for the Humanities Grant.

1969   *Anonymous Sins* (poems); *them* (novel); first prize, Emily

Clark Balch Short Story Competition, for "Convalescing";
second prize, O. Henry Prize Awards, for "Accomplished
Desires."

1970   *Love and Its Derangements* (poems); *The Wheel of Love* (stor-
ies); "Sunday Dinner" (play) premiered at American Place
Theatre, New York City; National Book Award for *them;*
Special Award for continuing achievement, O. Henry Prize
Awards.

1971–1972   Lived in London, England.

1971   *Wonderland* (novel).

1972   *The Edge of Impossibility* (essays); *Marriages and Infidelities*
(stories); "Ontological Proof of My Existence" (play) premiered at Cubiculo Theatre, New York City; second prize,
O. Henry Prize Awards for "Saul Bird Says: Relate! Communicate! Liberate!" (also entitled "Pilgrims' Progress").

1973   *Angel Fire* (poems); *Dreaming America* (poems); *Do With
Me What You Will* (novel); "Miracle Play" (play) pre-
miered at Playhouse II Theatre, New York City; first prize,
O. Henry Prize Awards for "The Dead."

1974   *The Goddess and Other Women* (stories); *New Heaven, New
Earth* (essays); *The Hungry Ghosts* (stories); *Miracle Play*
(play); *Where Are You Going, Where Have You Been?*
(stories).

1975   *The Assassins* (novel); *The Fabulous Beasts* (poems); *The Poisoned Kiss* (stories); *The Seduction* (stories); Lotus Club
Award of Merit.

1976   *Crossing the Border* (stories); *The Triumph of the Spider Monkey* (novella); *Childwold* (novel).

1977   *Night-Side* (stories).

1978   *Son of the Morning* (novel); *Women Whose Lives Are Food,
Men Whose Lives Are Money* (poems). Is elected to the
American Academy and Institute of Arts and Letters; at-
tends Soviet-American Writers Conference, New York City;
moves to New Jersey as writer-in-residence at Princeton
University.

1979   *Cybele* (novel); *Unholy Loves* (novel); *All the Good People I've
Left Behind* (stories).

1980   *Bellefleur* (novel); *A Sentimental Education* (stories); *Three Plays* (plays). Visits Europe, including Poland and Hungary, under auspices of the U.S. Information Agency.

1981   *Angel of Light* (novel); *Contraries* (essays).

1982   *A Bloodsmoor Romance* (novel); *Invisible Women* (poems).

1983   *The Profane Art* (essays).

1984   *Mysteries of Winterthurn* (novel); *Last Days* (stories). *Presque Isle* (play) is produced in New York at Theatre of the Open Eye.

1985   *Solstice* (novel); *Triumph of the Spider Monkey* (play) is produced at the Los Angeles Theatre Center.

1986   *Marya* (novel); *Raven's Wing* (stories). Wins O. Henry Award for Continuing Achievement.

1987   *You Must Remember This* (novel); *Lives of the Twins* (novel, under pseudonym); *On Boxing* (essay). Is made Roger S. Berlind Distinguished Professor in the Humanities at Princeton University.

1988   *The Assignation* (stories); *(Woman) Writer* (essays). Wins St. Louis Literary Award.

1989   *American Appetites* (novel); *Soul/Mate* (novel, under pseudonym); *The Time Traveler* (poems).

1990   *Because It Is Bitter, and Because It Is My Heart* (novel); *Nemesis* (novel, under pseudonym). *In Darkest America* (two plays) premiere at New Play Festival, Louisville—one of these plays, *The Eclipse,* is produced at the Ensemble Studio Theater, New York City. Receives Rea Award for the Short Story and Alan Swallow Award for *The Assignation.*

Chapter One

"The 'I,' which doesn't exist, is everything"

Personal and Cultural Contexts

In a 1988 essay, "Does the Writer Exist?," Joyce Carol Oates is bemused by the often disorienting "contrast between what we *know* of a writer from his or her work—the private self—and what we are forced to *confront* in the irrefutable flesh—the 'public' self."[1] Certainly, the contrast between Joyce Smith, the seemingly quiet, serene, cultivated, and sensitive woman, and Joyce Carol Oates, who writes of violence, brutality, sordidness, sexual compulsion, and emotional duress, has often struck observers.

Earlier, she carefully guarded the life and self that exist outside of her written work. Only the baldest facts were revealed. In recent years Oates has been somewhat less self-protective, letting out more information about her family background, acknowledging the autobiographical underpinnings of her works, commenting about personal experiences.

We can now fill in more about the "powerful appeal of certain personalities" and places in her life. Among the most potent influences are her parents and the "vanished world" of their lives and her childhood: "To say *my father, my mother* is for me to name but in no way to approach one of the central mysteries of my life."[2] Oates is more explicit about how much her writing is an attempt, in part, "to memorialize my parents' vanished world; my parents' lives. Sometimes directly, sometimes in metaphor." She goes back actually and psychically into her family's past in her recent writing. There is a coming-home quality—a reappraisal of the past from the mellow perspective of midlife—about Oates's latest work, which is more openly autobiographical and personal. She went back to the realm of her childhood, for example, to prepare to write the novel *Marya: A Life* (1986), which is, she acknowledges, a deliberate conflation of her mother's experiences and her own. Similarly, in *You Must Remember This* (1987), she claims to have "tried consciously to synthesize my father's and my own 'visions' of an era now vanished" ("Father," 84).

Oates is bemused by the "genteel" literary community that misunder-

1

stands and criticizes the harsh and violent world of much of her fiction. This world, Oates insists, is part of her literal and psychic inheritance. She tells of the tremendous tension she experienced writing *Marya*, "the most 'personal' of my novels." She had the feeling that she was "trespassing— transgressing?—in some undefined way venturing onto forbidden ground." She discovers belatedly that she had fictionally recapitulated an incident from her family's past that had not been disclosed to her: the murder of her maternal grandfather in a barroom brawl, after which her mother was "given away" to be reared by her aunt's family.[3] In an uncanny way, she was drawn to invent (or to remember) this subject from her family's past.

There are other violent events and family secrets only recently revealed. Oates's paternal grandfather, Joseph Carlton Oates, abandoned her grandmother and father when her father was only two. Twenty-eight years later he reappeared, bearing a grudge against his son, wanting to fight him, but the son, Frederick Oates, would not participate. Joyce Carol Oates comments sardonically that perhaps the most unintentionally generous gesture of her grandfather was his abandonment of his family, for "it is likely, given his penchant for drinking and aggressive behavior, he might very well have been abusive to his wife and to my father, would surely have 'beaten him up' many times—so infecting him, if we are to believe current theories of the etiology of domestic violence, with a similar predisposition toward violence." Oates learned recently that when her father was 15 her great-grandfather tried unsuccessfully to kill his wife in a fit of rage and then killed himself ("Father," 45, 84).

While her father did not duplicate the violent patterns of behavior of his father and grandfather, he was fascinated with the "romance of violence" and its transmutation into masculine sport, "which excludes women," and he retained a "conviction that there is a mysterious and terrible brotherhood of men by way of violence." He took his daughter to boxing matches, inculcating in her the same lifelong fascination with the sport (and with violence). For her, however, as we shall see, boxing is a study of "the other": "Boxing is for men, and is about men, and *is* men."[4] Frederick Oates also enjoyed another quintessentially "male" sport, flying—the "romance of the air," as Oates calls it, "transcending space and time and the contours of the familiar world in which you work a minimum of 40 hours a week, own property in constant need of repair, have a family for whom you are the sole breadwinner[.] What is flying but the control of an alien, mysterious element that can at any moment turn killer—the air?" He and his flying buddies performed loops and turns and rolls, and sometimes buzzed friends' and neighbors' houses. It was her father, Oates claims, who inspired the flying scenes in her novel *Bellefleur* (1980). He also sometimes took his young daughter Joyce for rides ("Father," 84–85), which appears, curiously, to have precipitated the fear of flying that compelled the adult Oates to eschew air travel whenever possible.

What most impresses Oates about her father and mother is their representative and exemplary survival and "transcendence" of "a world so harsh and so repetitive in its harshness as to defy evocation, except perhaps in art" ("Father," 84). They survived and prevailed despite family turmoil and the wrenching hardships and dislocations of the Great Depression. Her mother, creative with flowers and in decorating the house, still makes her daughter's clothes. Her father, who had to quit high school, who was laid off work several times, and who worked most of his life as a tool-and-die designer, has innate musical ability and, at over 70 years of age, enrolled in classes in English literature and music at the State University of New York at Buffalo.

They are neither self-pitying nor nostalgic about the hard times of the past. Of her father Oates writes, "If there was anger it's long since buried, plowed under, to be resurrected in his daughter's writing, as fuel and ballast." That Oates is, for example, the first member of her family to graduate from high school, let alone college, evokes in her a "class" anger, but she makes clear that it is "a personal anger, not one I have inherited from my family." From her parents Oates claims to have learned the genius of happiness, an "instinct for rejoicing in the life in which they have found themselves," and a predilection for useful employment: "we love to work because work gives us genuine happiness, the positing and solving of problems, the joyful exercise of the imagination" ("Father," 108).

What is critical in understanding Oates's relationship to American traditions and culture, I believe, is that she sees her parents' lives, and her own, as emblematically American. Her parents' survival and triumph over hardship —and, similarly, her own "transmogrification" of their vanished world into art—are examples of the aspiring and triumphant human spirit.

Oates's family is prototypically American in its multicultural immigrant origins: Irish, German, and Hungarian. Her maternal grandparents were Hungarians who emigrated to the United States in ship steerage at the turn of the century and settled in the Buffalo area.[5] Her grandfather's name was Bús, Americanized to Bush; her grandmother's name was Torony. She says, "I never read Upton Sinclair's *The Jungle* without a powerful reaction; surely Sinclair was describing my grandparents' lives as well as those of his hapless Lithuanian immigrants." She was raised "American" with most of what was ethnic "ignored, or denied, or repressed, very likely for reasons of necessity." The temperament of her Hungarian grandfather, for example, might seem

to "sound flamboyant and colorful" only "if seen through the retrospective
of years and the prudent filter of language." Similarly, her grandmother's
refusal to learn to read English, reasoning that it was "too late" when she
had come to the States at age 16, although she lived into her eighties, "is associated in my mind with a peculiar sort of Old World obstinacy and self-
defeat." There was no contact for over 60 years with relatives in Hungary,
and she and her brother[6] learned no Hungarian as children. Yet when she
visited Budapest in May of 1980, she experienced a kind of unsettling recognition. For one thing, she is "struck by the disquietingly familiar look of
strangers glimpsed on the streets: the eyes, the cheekbones, skin coloring,
the general bearing." Some resemble her, she thinks, more than her brother
or parents: "Uncanny sensation!—as if I had stepped into a dream." She is
disoriented by the realization that Joyce Carol Oates is widely read in
Hungary—another indication, no doubt, of uncanny correspondence. Most
dominant is the visceral "tug of recognition, pleasurable yet disturbing"
with the people: "I have been told that beneath their gaiety Hungarians are
melancholy people and of course it's true: I know the temperament from
within" ("Budapest," 331–35).

Budapest is one of the memorable cities that engraves itself on the author's psyche. "Lovely Budapest": I don't know where I am, but I think I
am at home" ("Budapest," 343). Oates's experiences while on tour in
Eastern-bloc countries inspired some fine stories, such as "Old Budapest"
and "My Warszawa: 1980" in her volume of short stories *Last Days* (1984).

Indeed, the shaping effect of place is critical to an understanding of Joyce
Carol Oates. The quintessential world of her fiction remains the geography
of her childhood—both the countryside around Millersport in upper New
York State, where she lived on her grandparents' farm, and the small city,
Lockport, where she attended school. The latter locale becomes her fictitious and symbolic Eden County, akin to Faulkner's "little postage stamp
world," Yoknapatawpha County. This Eden County world is skillfully
evoked in a number of works, from her first, such as *By the North Gate*
(1963), *Upon the Sweeping Flood* (1966), and *With Shuddering Fall*
(1964), through her most recent, including: *Son of the Morning* (1978),
Bellefleur, Marya: A Life, You Must Remember This, and *Because It Is Bitter,
and Because It Is My Heart* (1990). Oates's childhood world remains the
generating core of her fiction, infusing her work with resonance and
authenticity.

Lockport, with its distinctive Erie Canal, Oates explains, is "the city of
my birth, my paternal grandmother's home, suffused forever for me with
the extravagant dreams of early adolescence—I attended sixth grade in

Lockport, and all of junior high school there; the city is probably more real to me, imaginatively, than any I have known since."[7] Lockport is sometimes, as in *Marya,* imagined as "Innisfail," evoking Yeats's lost romantic world. Sometimes, as in *You Must Remember This,* Lockport becomes fused with another city of Oates's experience, Buffalo, to become the fictitious city "Port Oriskany." Oates claims to have had a map of Port Oriskany taped to her wall during the writing of *You Must Remember This* so that she could stare at it and "traverse its streets, ponder its buildings and houses and vacant lots, most of all that canal that runs through it" (Preface to *Y,* 380).

Not only is the Eden County world described with authenticity, so also is the quintessential Oatesian experience associated with that place: female adolescence. Repeatedly in her stories and novels, Oates portrays with convincing resonance the inchoate identity of the adolescent girl who plays alternatively at being good and being wild. Oates captures so well the dreamy narcissism of the adolescent, her infatuation with sleazy charms, her experimental flirtation with danger, temptation, and even death.

Second only to the world of her childhood is the impact of Detroit on the writer. Detroit is, Oates acknowledges, the place "which made me the person I am, consequently the writer I am—for better or worse." She acknowledges that much of the writing of her early period, between 1963 and 1976, "has been emotionally inspired by Detroit and its suburbs (Birmingham, Bloomfield Hills, to a lesser degree Grosse Pointe) that it is impossible for me now to extract the historical from the fictional."[8]

In an essay entitled "Visions of Detroit" she asks: "Why do some events, some people, some landscapes urban or rural fall upon us with an almost inhuman authority, dictating the terms of our most private fantasies, forcing upon us what amounts very nearly to a second birth—while others, most others, make virtually no impression at all and quickly fade." There's "never an answer," she concludes; but she does think, in retrospect, that "the extraordinary emotional impact Detroit had" on her must have been partly due to the awakening of "submerged memories of childhood and adolescence in and around the equally 'great' city of Buffalo, New York" ("Detroit," 348).

Detroit has, for Joyce Carol Oates, a representational and visceral effect: she characterizes it as "ceaseless motion, the pulse of the city. The beat. The beat. A place of romance, the quintessential American city." Its "brooding presence, a force, larger and more significant than the sum of its parts" offered "a sentimental education never to be repeated for me" ("Detroit," 347, 349). For those of us who, like Oates, have lived in Detroit, she does indeed convincingly evoke the city—its streets and neighborhoods, its institutions, its geographical and social stratifications, its raw and seamy violence, its vaguely threatening but hauntingly vital "pulse."

Detroit offered Oates a vivid canvas on which to explore the "larger social/political/moral implications of my characters' experiences."[9] While detailing the lives of specific characters, Oates's novels encapsulate important phenomena of American culture: the migration of poor to the city, like the Wendalls in *them* (1969); the sterility of the suburban rich, as in *Expensive People* (1968); the effects of social upheavals such as the Detroit riot in *them;* and the malaise of the sixties, as in *Wonderland* (1971). A number of Detroit novels look critically at major societal institutions— medicine, law, education—and the struggles of radically dislocated characters who look to these structures for stable concepts of identity. Most often a male character dominates the early Oates novel, and the central movement of the novel is his attempt to free himself from intolerable constraints, often through violence—a mode of action particularly suited to Detroit, the reigning "murder capitol."

Joyce Carol Oates observes the gaudy drama of this prototypical city from her comparatively serene and protected residence in the university. The university, in fact, is another important place in Oates's fictional world. All of her adulthood—from age 17 on—Oates has lived within the culture of a university. Yet for a significant period of Oates's career, the university is dwarfed by the city. The conflict between the city and the university, between the demands of the raw external environment and the lures of the seemingly protected world of academia, is an important tension in Oates's work: it is a conflict played out in her Detroit fiction as well as in her later works.

Sister Irene in "In the Region of Ice" (*The Wheel of Love,* 1970) cannot minister to the raging emotional needs of her student, Allen Weinstein. Maureen in *them* accuses her teacher "Joyce Carol Oates" of being off in a world of books, unaware of the demands of the world in which her students live. Maureen has throughout her harsh young life looked to the library and books quite literally as a sanctuary from reality, and she sets out on a quest to beg, borrow, and steal her way into the protected environment of academia: she becomes, through determined husband-stealing, the wife of a college instructor. The university is vaguely implicated in the social unrest of the sixties: Jules Wendall becomes part of the foolish-sounding, incendiary counterculture around Wayne State University at the time of the Detroit riot.

Others of Oates's characters are not peripheral hangers-on but legitimate students who attempt to make themselves anew within a university culture, such as Jesse (*Wonderland*) in his medical studies at the University of Michigan. He, like Marya in a much later book, discovers that it is not easy to slough off the past and construct a new self.

Sometimes the academic world itself becomes the central setting of Oates's work: it is not portrayed sympathetically. In *The Hungry Ghosts* (1974), set at "Hilberry University" in southwestern Ontario (and probably inspired by Oates's experiences at the University of Windsor), Oates takes a satiric perspective, stressing the insecurities, pedantry, fears, and phobias within a claustrophobic academic culture. That satiric perspective continues with another academic fiction, *Unholy Loves* (1979), set at "Woodslee University" in upper New York State, although the novel is also a serious study of the "holy love" of art, and the validity and sanctity of the artist's vocation.

Increasingly, Joyce Carol Oates's fiction is about the attractions and the dangers of the life of the mind, and gradually women take central stage. Whereas a number of Oates's early novels focus on male protagonists and their quests for liberation from intolerable constraints, often through violence, the novels of Oates's middle period portray a number of intelligent, gifted, sensitive young women, who are more identifiably like the author herself: Laney in *Childwold* (1976), Brigit in *Unholy Loves,* Monica and Sheila of *Solstice* (1985), Marya in *Marya: A Life,* Enid in *You Must Remember This,* Iris in *Because It Is Bitter, and Because It Is My Heart*—not to mention the more fanciful characterizations of Deidre in *A Bloodsmoor Romance* (1982), and Perdita in *Mysteries of Winterthurn* (1984).

Oates circles back to her childhood world as she depicts more frequently young women with a developing interest in books and ideas—an interest sharply at odds with the tough, mindless, back-country environment in which many of them are situated. Some of the bright young girls of Oates's fictional world find genuine, if fitful, joy in their awakening to the inner life. They go far beyond the vacuous and frightened women of Oates's earlier fiction—the Maureen Wendalls who try to steal their way into the academic world, to cocoon themselves from the harshness of the external world.

For example, Kasch in *Childwold* describes Laney's awakening: "You stir, you wake, you come to consciousness, heaved upon the sands of consciousness; but where are you, why have you gone so far? The books you read are not my books, the language you use is not my language."[10] *Marya* describes the formative awakening of a young girl's intellectual life at a university. Marya—like Enid, Brigit, and Sheila—is also drawn to the artistic life and to the attractions and the dangers of the unconscious, the generating source of creativity. Oates depicts in these young women the developing sensibilities of the female artist. Portrayed, as well, is the uneasy residence of the artistic sensibility within the academy, the conflicting pulls of the conscious and the unconscious, the intellectual and the instinctual—conflicts that are dramatized, for example, in the symbiotic relationship of the artist and teacher, Sheila and Monica, in *Solstice*.

Since Oates both literally and figuratively lives within a university culture —now that of Princeton University, where she is the Roger S. Berlind Distinguished Professor in the Humanities—it is not surprising that her work, both creative and critical, is very much informed by and set within the context of intellectual traditions. While Oates is at times critical of the academy, its failed teachers, its fears and phobias and petty politics, she is also very aware of its value: its sanctification of the inner life, its rich heritage of ideas and art. A distinguished teacher; a learned critic; a provocative and insightful reviewer and commentator; a coeditor, along with her husband, Raymond Smith, of the *Ontario Review* and the Ontario Review Press; a major writer of novels, stories, plays, and poems: Oates is indeed, as John Updike has suggested, aptly described as a "woman of letters."[11]

Conceptual and Aesthetic Contexts

It is the mature woman of letters, the Joyce Carol Oates within her published work, about whom I am most concerned in this study of the novels of the middle years. Where does this voice fit within intellectual and literary traditions? Oates's provocative and astute critical essays continue to offer both valuable insights into her views of the artistic process and useful perspectives from which to view her fiction.

Subscribing to romantic and modernist logocentrism, Oates argues in her critical essays that the author's voice and vision are encapsulated in a work of art. Not for her is the postmodern view that "texts" (which she calls "that most sinister of terms")[12] unravel, deconstruct on the page. Rather, "the greatest works of art sometimes strike us as austere and timeless, self-contained and self-referential, with their own private music, as befits sacred things."[13] Reading is "the sole means by which we slip, involuntarily, often helplessly, into another's skin; another's voice; another's soul." As writing is a search for the "sacred text," criticism is "the profane art," the "art of reflection upon reflection . . . [a] discursive commentary upon another's vision."[14] In direct challenge to poststructuralist theories that would "decenter" the author, Joyce Carol Oates insists on the essentially rhetorical and pleasurable nature of writing and of reading: art provides an opportunity for communication between the consciousness of the writer and the reader.

Oates is unconcerned about the "anxiety of influence" described by Harold Bloom. An erudite person, she readily acknowledges, "I've been influenced in many ways by nearly everyone I've read, and I've read nearly everyone."[15] But Oates does not take the structuralist view that devalues the individual and asserts the primacy of external shaping forces (language, culture, history). Rather, she retains (to be sure, with some skepticism and questioning) the romantic notion of the uniqueness and the primacy of the individual.

The private, fluid, ultimately mysterious core of the self is a subject of bemused speculation in a number of Oates's essays and fictional works. In a 1984 essay she looks back to a time in 1972 and comments that "I seemed to have been another person, related to the person I am now as one is related, tangentially, sometimes embarrassingly, to cousins not seen for decades." Yet she claims to have had then, while very sick, a "mystical vision." Although now the very term seems "such pretension," the experience impressed her enormously. She envisioned

the "body" [as] a tall column of light and blood heat, a temporary agreement among atoms, like a high-rise building with numberless rooms, corridors, corners, elevators shafts, windows. . . . In this fantastical structure the "I" is deluded as to its sovereignty, let alone its autonomy in the (outside) world; the most astonishing secret is that the "I" doesn't exist!—but it behaves as if it does, as if it were one and not many. In any case, without the "I" the tall column of light and heat would die, and the microscopic life particles would die with it . . . will die with it. The "I," which doesn't exist, is everything.[16]

So, the deluded sovereignty of the nonexistent "I" is a matter of some irony to Oates, and she equates this irony with a postmodern perspective: "as a novelist of the 1980s, my vision is postmodernist, and therefore predisposed to irony" ("Pleasure," 197). Yet her postmodern irony does not discredit the intellectual and literary heritage of humanism and modernism. The elusive self, "individual, stubborn, self-reliant, and ultimately mysterious," is at the center of Oates's work. *Marya* (1986), for example, is prefaced by a quotation from William James—"My first act of freedom is to believe in freedom"—and the spirit of James, Oates says, pervades the novel. What she says about James's views is equally applicable to her own: "It is the fluidity of experience and not its Platonic 'essence' that is significant, for truth is relative, ever-changing, indeterminate; and life is a process rather like a stream. Human beings forge their own souls by way of the choices they make, large and small, conscious and half-conscious. . . . identity (social, historical, familial) is not permanent" (Preface to *M*, 377–78).

Oates's perspective, then, is very human-centered. Only with human consciousness, human perception, human creativity is the world given significance. For her it is not an overstatement to say, along with Emily Dickinson, "The Brain—is wider than the Sky—." She argues that "most human beings, writers or not, are in disguise as their outward selves . . . their truest and most valuable selves are interior" ("Exist," 52). But the interior self is dualistic, made up of both conscious and unconscious contents, and ideally what needs to be achieved is some happy balance between the two: "that mysterious integration of the personality that has its theological analogue in the concept of grace."[17]

Joyce Carol Oates sounds very Jungian when she argues that the psyche "seems to be at its fullest when contradictory forces are held in suspension" ("Soul," 185). Like Jung, Oates has a tremendous respect for the dark other within the self. It is out of the human psyche that all that is mysterious has arisen—all the wonderlands perpetuated across time, all the Jekyll/Hyde dualities, all the collective fantasies we call culture.[18] There are intimations of a Jungian collective unconsciousness in some of Oates's remarks, or at the very least a recognition of universal commonalities in human experience, and especially in American cultural experience. The artist is exceptionally receptive to them as they well up, with their own undeniable authority, out of the unconscious: "Something *not us* inhabits us; something insists upon speaking through us" ("Beginnings," 14).

Just as the self is ideally balanced between conscious and unconscious contents, so too does the writer attempt to achieve a balance between unconscious motives and conscious technique. Technique—"the dams, dikes, ditches, and conduits that both restrain emotionally charged content and give it formal, and therefore communal, expression"[19]—act as the writer's defense against the "white heat" of the unconscious: "Clearly the powerful unconscious motives for a work of art are but the generating and organizing forces that stimulate consciousness to feats of deliberation, strategy, craft, cunning." Oates describes her own practice as a writer as "an active pursuit of 'hauntedness': I can't write unless I am preoccupied with something sometimes to the point of distraction or obsession." Being in the grip of a literary obsession "has the force of something inhuman: primitive, almost impersonal, at time almost frightening" ("Beginnings," 7, 19, 14).

Oates, raised a Catholic, appears to have no belief in a transcendent God, but she does subscribe to a sense of immanent (albeit metaphoric) godliness within the inner life, the human psyche: "To say that the kingdom of God is within is, in one sense, to speak simply in metaphor, and very simply. To say that most people are very rarely interested in the kingdom of God (at least as it lies within, and not without) is to speak the most obvious truth." Oates places the highest possible value on the godlike creativity of the artist: it is not outrageous to think that "we live the lives we live in order to produce the art of which we believe ourselves capable" ("Soul," 172, 177).

In her repeated borrowing of theological metaphors to describe the nature of art, Oates echoes the high modernist tradition of Joyce and Yeats: "The secret at the heart of all creative activity has something to do with our desire to complete a work, to impose perfection upon it, so that, hammered out of profane materials, it becomes sacred: which is to say, no longer merely personal" ("Dream," 43).

To achieve such a sacred text is a kind of triumph, a transcendence of the profane. Throughout her work, Oates is concerned with transcendence of various kinds, with human attempts to overcome limitations and obstacles. "Can it be true, or is it a useful fiction," she asks, "that the cosmos is created anew in the individual?—that one can, by way of a defiant act of self-begetting, transcend the fate of the nation, the community, the family, and —for a woman—the socially determined parameters of gender?"[20] Her characters are groping toward wholeness, struggling to grow. She says, "in my fiction, the troubled people are precisely those who yearn for a higher life—those in whom the life-form itself is stirring. . . . only out of restlessness can higher personalities emerge, just as, in a social context, it is only out of occasional surprises and upheavals that new ways of life can emerge" (Boesky, 482).

To be sure, the difficulty of such transcendence is dramatized again and again in Oates's fiction: she is aware of the hubris, the Faustian overreaching, that is often a part of such a struggle. Moreover, her characters are deeply embedded within entangling familial and social groups, and within recognizably American geographical, historical, cultural, political, and ethical contexts. Oates claims that she "could not take the time to write about a group of people who did not represent, in their various struggles, fantasies, unusual experiences, hopes, etc., our society in miniature" (Boesky, 482).

In her faith in the aspiring human spirit, Oates is prototypically American and finds her place within the traditions of American romanticism. But it is romanticism with a difference, with an ironic postmodernist recognition that "the 'I,' which doesn't exist, is everything." She says, "Our past may weight heavily upon us but it cannot contain us, let alone shape our future. America is a tale still being told—in many voices—and nowhere near its conclusion."[21] She herself—the Joyce Carol Oates who doesn't exist in the flesh but who is a voice incarnated in an impressive body of work—is one of the preeminent tellers of that tale.

Chapter Two

Holy and Unholy Loves: God, Art, Sex, Goodness

While in many ways radically dissimilar, the four novels of Oates's early middle years—*Son of the Morning, Unholy Loves, Cybele,* and *Angel of Light*—have in common their portrayal of love-madness, a holy or unholy love obsessing the central character. They bring a range of perspectives—sympathetic to satiric—to bear on a common Oatesian theme, the hunger to transcend human limitations through the redemptive powers of love. These are romantic quests, fraught with pitfalls and delusion, and intermingled with the baser emotions: self-absorption, pride, lust, greed, ambition. Each novel demonstrates that the physicality of human existence cannot be denied or transcended, yet not all of these quests are failures: the aspiring spirit, although often entangled in self-delusion, sometimes finds redemption.

Son of the Morning

Oates once said, "a redefinition of God in terms of the furtherest reaches of man's hallucinations can provide us with a new basis for tragedy."[1] *Son of the Morning* (1978) is about those tragic hallucinations. In preparation for writing the book, Oates immersed herself in the culture of American evangelical religion: "I wanted to put myself in the place of a fundamentalist Protestant who would not have any critical or historical preconceptions . . . getting into that frame of mind was a very shattering experience."[2]

The religious mysticism of the central character, Nathanael (Nathan) Vickery, has validity at the same time that it is a delusion fed by willful narcissism. What Oates has said about religious mystics in general (and about Simone Weil in particular) applies equally well to Nathanael:

The mystic experiences a powerful subjective reorganization of his psyche, and the experience is certainly valid. But that it has reference to an entity casually called The Universe is extremely doubtful. One reads Weil, then, with a variety of emotions. Fascination at first. Exasperation. Disappointment. Even anger at her willfulness, her refusal to recognize her own narcissism though she is quick to see it in others. . . . In the end one feels a certain suspense, as in the reading of a good novel: will the heroine wake from her delusion in time to save her life?"³

Nathanael does not wake up from his delusion to save his life, even though his mystical vision fails him.

The novel begins at the end with the voice of lament, of incantation, a pleading for reunion with God. We learn that the voice is that of the adult Nathanael, who feels irrevocably severed from his earlier self, who had been blissfully one with God since birth: "The child Nathanael dwelled with God, and there was no time when he was not with God. So it was: before his birth and afterward. He knew not the terrible loneliness that I and many others, fallen from Your regard, have known."⁴

Conceived through the rape of his "virgin" mother Elsa—an ironically inverted Immaculate Conception—Nathan is brought up by his religious grandmother and his atheist grandfather. His grandmother, who tells him of God and takes him to religious services, is soon convinced he has extraordinary powers. At age five he experiences the first of seven revelations "when God seize[s] him in the flesh" (*SM*, 88). He handles a copperhead snake during the service of a backcountry preacher. His grandfather is skeptical, scornful, and critical of both his grandson's alleged visions and the biblical "Jesus of Nazareth who was vindictive, crafty, sly, opportunistic, hypocritical. But, most of all bullying. Cruel and sadistic and bullying. Hateful" (*SM*, 135). At the end of book one the grandfather dies of a massive stroke, apparently occasioned by the glaring light refracted off a knife Nathanael was using in the kitchen. Symbolically, he is struck down by the "light of Christ" embodied in Nathanael.

The next book of *Son of the Morning*, "The Witness," details Nathanael's singleminded dedication to God and to his growing fame as an evangelical preacher. His obsessive, uncompromising, unforgiving faith is played off against the lax, lazy, worldly Christianity of Reverend Beloff, an evangelical syndicated-television preacher akin to modern-day entrepreneurial preachers such as Jim Bakker and Jimmy Swaggart. Beloff's lusty life of seduction of parishioners is complemented with a handy doctrine of constant baptism, in which sins are washed away. He finds the religious profession lucrative: "The American people are not tight-fisted and suspicious . . . They are naturally charitable; they *want* to give. But where are the organizations worthy of their generosity? The pity is, there are so few" (*SM*, 215).

Nathanael, in contrast, doesn't want money or brotherhood or love or individual happiness: he wants only oneness with God. He is a driven, obsessive personality: fanatical, rigid, willful, unforgiving. His stony certitude in interpreting the Bible; his biblical intonations; his childlike, shameless emotion; his total sincerity; his single-mindedness make him an extremely charismatic preacher who inspires a considerable following.

For him God's existence is real, and everything else is ephemeral and insignificant: "Christ existed, Christ was certainly more than a vapor. But Nathan could not be sure whether he himself existed, and whether other people existed. The flesh was ephemeral, after all" (*SM*, 175). He attempts to reject the flesh entirely: "I'm spirit. We're all spirit. . . . Bodies are insignificant. . . . The Spirit of the Lord is not material" (*SM*, 223), he insists. In his view it is the Devil who gives sexual feelings, who blinds people to their spiritual nature. The Devil isn't a person but "a way of seeing."

But Nathanael, for all his imperiousness, is still human and not immune to the Devil. When Leonie Beloff's flirtation with him evokes a carnal response, he is disgusted by his God-obliterating lust: "His lust for her was perverse. It frightened him. He wondered at times if he were going insane. For it was insanity, wasn't it, for one of God's creatures to desire another so violently that God Himself was obliterated—?" (*SM*, 180).

The God of Leonie and her father, Reverend Beloff, is tough—a mighty fortress—and forgiving: "There ain't anything much you can do to injure *Him*. You can turn and walk away and come crawling back on your hands and knees, and He's just gonna pick you up in the palm of His mighty hand a give a good chuckle, you know?" (*SM*, 183). But the God of Nathanael is implacable, unforgiving, punishing.

Nathanael has horrific visions—akin to those of Jonathan Edwards or Stephen Dedalus—of terrible tortures awaiting human beings who "sinned with their flesh, and turned away" from God. One such vision climaxes in a desolate view of the world with totally dehumanized flesh devouring flesh: "No life could endure here; yet there were people on all sides, fighting one another even as they gasped for breath. Arms and legs coiled snake-like; heads fought bodies. There were jaws without faces, double rows of teeth that tore and devoured. What a clawing, pummeling, moaning, panting, writhing, shrieking! The air rocked with delirium . . . 'There is no help for those whom God has abandoned,' Christ said" (*SM*, 159). Moreover, God warns Nathanael about his own grave danger, his own sinful pride: "'All that you have seen, Nathan, will be as nothing compared to the sorrow that will be yours,' Christ whispered, 'for you are guilty of the sin of pride'" (*SM*, 160).

It is little wonder, then, that Nathanael is as uncompromising as his God. Finally, on Good Friday, so obsessed with his own lust and pride,

Nathanael—recalling Flannery O'Connor's and Nathanael West's God-obsessed self-tormenters—turns to a drastic expedient: he plucks out one of his eyes before the stunned congregation, declaring "that so public an act was sinful in itself, and that its grotesque exhibitionism would be—when he recalled it in later life—part of his humiliation." Yet "God Himself" had ordained this ceremony. Nathan must be punished, he must be broken and humiliated publicly, for he had embarked upon a public career in God's name, and God was very displeased, and must now be placated" (*SM,* 235).

The third book of *Son of the Morning,* "Last Things," details more explicitly the present time of the narration of the book. Nathanael, holed up in a small room in midwinter, retrospectively tries to "re-imagine" the Nathanael Vickery before the "fall," before he had become irrevocably separated from God—a task "far more difficult . . . than I had anticipated" (*SM,* 272). We learn that he had returned to his ministry after the melodramatic blinding of one eye on Good Friday, that the incident had only served to call more attention to him. He travels 25,000 miles, visits 80 cities, is seen by millions of people in person and on television.

But Nathanael's success is irrelevant to him; he is totally absorbed in God. "Nothing matters except God: nothing. Not war, not struggle, not poverty, not disappointments, not physical or mental anguish; not the deaths of oneself or one's family: not even happiness. Most of all it was happiness, Vickery exclaimed, that tempted man away from God" (*SM,* 252). He holds himself in readiness for God, exists only for God, lives from one revelation to another, even though these visions are far apart: "eight years were to pass between your manifestation on the eve of Good Friday, 1959, and the fifth of your manifestations in late September of 1967" (*SM,* 286).

It is the fifth vision that is the most spectacular—the vision of "The One: The Spirit of Absolute Illumination: the Many-in-One: You" (*SM,* 287). In this vision God both appears and disappears; He demonstrates both his power of creation and that of extinction. Nathanael witnesses "the extinction of Christ, His form blasted into its elements and then reassembled, sucked in and out of existence, and his kinship with Christ was therefore a terrible one: they were linked not in their power but in their powerlessness" (*SM,* 296).

Nathanael's separation from God is brought out by a final terrifying vision in front of a crowd when "[God] allowed him to know that [His] love for him was at an end. Quite suddenly, after so many years—it was over" (*SM,* 61). It is then that Nathanael sees for the first time the face of God. It is a terrible deflation of expectation: "a great hole. A great mouth . . . and

. . . the writhing dancing molecules of flesh were being sucked into it, and ground to nothing, and at the same time retained their illusory being. What he knew to be You [God] before him imagined itself quite otherwise— imagined itself broken and separated into parts, into individuals, into people, "men" and "women" and "children." It was madness, their madness, Your madness, and he was paralyzed before it" (*SM*, 362). Nathanael's final vision is thus of God as the physical processes of life: nothing more or less than a great, ravenous mouth. Oates repeatedly confronts her soaring spiritualists with the reality of the implacable, impersonal, and deflating organism of life. In *The Assassins* (1975), for example, Yvonne's recurrent nightmare involves the breakup of her carpet into corpses seething with maggots, dramatizing the deathliness of her human control and the implacability of the life feeding on life. Nathan's Dantesque "writhing dancing molecules of flesh" before God's "ravenous mouth" is yet another shocking image of the unredeemed physical life.

This devastating revelation throws Nathanael into a "death-trance," and the final book of the novel, "Epilogue: The Sepulcher," shows him to be broken, wounded, and utterly baffled by his fate. He has rebaptized himself "William Vickery" in a mock ceremony on the banks of the Eden River. But he remains uncompromising, uninterested in life in the world. He cannot dismiss the oneness with God that he experienced for a time; he cannot accept ordinary life: "Man's hunger for God . . . cannot be satisfied by earthly food. Don't speak to me of 'human' love. Don't speak to me of 'making a place for oneself' here: It is quite pointless. It is not even cruel: only pointless" (*SM*, 378). The novel ends with his perpetual wait: "So I wait for You, and will wait the rest of my life" (*SM*, 382).

Nathanael Vickery is Oates's most extended treatment of the God-obsessed, but he is a type that has appeared before in her novels: other notable examples are Stephen in *The Assassins* (1975), Mered Dawe in *Do With Me What You Will* (1973), and Jedediah in *Bellefleur.* Moreover, other characters have also been taken with the idea that they are, as Jules Wendall is described in *them,* "pure spirit struggling to break free of the morass of flesh. He thought of himself as spirit struggling with the fleshly earth, the very force of gravity, death."[5]

Oates herself, in essays and correspondence, has described herself as "in some vague way a 'religious' writer" in that she is interested in those "activities that take the individual out of his claustrophobic ego-role" (Boesky, 482). She writes of a "gradual transformation of Western culture" toward a kind of "intelligent pantheism" that includes "all substance in the universe (including the substance fortunate enough to perceive it)."[6]

An interesting twist to *Son of the Morning* is that it includes the character Japheth, an intellectual who becomes a disciple of Nathanael and who echoes some of Oates's own statements. He sees in the appeal of Nathanael's ministry to the middle class and the educated:

> the possibility of—of something wonderful, something marvelous—a revolution of consciousness . . . the United States might be on the brink of an entirely new consciousness: a revolution in Christ's name. . . . "It's my personal theory that—that the younger generation is turning aside from material things," Japheth said, "and—and from certain of the old cultural ideals—the worship of masculine competition and endless contests—the worship of masculine *virtue*—virility—I think we've come to the point in the evolution of our species where we're ready to—to make a leap to another—The cruelty of the Hellenistic ideal has had its day, after so many centuries: at least we can be brothers and sisters in Christ!" (*SM*, 321–23)

There are, of course, important distinctions to be made between the views of Japheth and Nathanael and between those of Oates and her characters. Whereas Oates's monistic vision synthesizes mind and matter into a kind of "higher humanism," Japheth's dualism rejects the mundane world for a transcendent spiritual realm: "The earthly must go its own way while I cast my life with the other. . . . The earthly, the mundane, the practical . . . the *sane* . . . Can't be taken seriously once one has tasted the other world" (*SM*, 301).

So too does Nathanael reject the physical world. But ironically, Nathanael ejects Japheth from the Seekers because he is convinced by a dream "revelation" that Japheth is physically, not spiritually, attracted to him: the Seekers' religion finds any emotional attraction suspect, a sign of debasing physicality. Later Japheth becomes unhinged and attempts unsuccessfully to kill Nathanael, convinced that Nathanael is indeed the "Son of God" who is ushering in the end of the world. Finally, Japheth commits suicide in a mental hospital.

Nathanael is uninterested in Japheth's intellectualizing of his ministry, his brotherhood in Christ. More and more convinced of his own godliness, Nathan is self-absorbed, arrogant, imperious, convinced of his infallibility, his invulnerability. His ego is not overcome; it grows massive. His pride soars before his fall, echoing Lucifer, that other son of the morning. As Nathanael takes up a healing ministry, he believes himself to be God incarnate: "Nathan Vickery, the Chosen One, was immortal: unkillable" (*SM*, 353). He becomes yet another of Oates's egotistical overreachers, characters whose solipsistic selves replace the world. He is not unlike Pederson and

Jesse in *Wonderland*. His is the ultimate hallucination: thinking he is God. He is set up for the ultimate deflation: the reduction of God to the impersonal, ravenous life process.

There is no godhead disconnected from life itself. Throughout, Oates takes care to set Nathanael's story within the context of the physical. The first scene of the novel depicts the savage hunting down and destruction of a rapacious pack of wild dogs, themselves characterized as "long stomachs." Here is nature, red in tooth and claw. That Nathanael was conceived in rape is a vivid reminder of his unredeemed physical origins.

Nathanael's extended lament, his wish for a reunion with God, is treated sympathetically. His retrospective questioning and longing are poignantly wrought. Why has God now abandoned him? Was he deceived about his earlier oneness with God? "Were you indeed present in the form of the Holy Spirit when Nathan performed his many cures?" (*SM*, 315). "God intoxicated am I, or only stubborn? Or defiant? Calling the one least like me, to the One Who has swallowed me up and forgotten me. Who gave birth to me, and devoured me, and excreted me into the drifting, clamoring world" (*SM*, 344).

The author has said that she felt an "absolute kinship" with the character, that the book is "painfully autobiographical, in part."[7] The need to find meaning in life, to transcend limitations, to be assured of one's special status is a persistent human obsession; the striving human spirit knows no restraint. But "the world has no meaning; I am sadly resigned to this fact," says the bemused author, who sets out to "sanctify the world." She rejects absolutism: "the world has meanings, many individual and alarming and graspable meanings, and the adventure of human beings consists in seeking out these meanings."[8] Some of those meanings are encapsulated in the tragedy of her deluded visionary Nathanael Vickery.

Unholy Loves

Although the love of God fails Nathanael Vickery, the love of art offers a kind of redemption and salvation to the central character of *Unholy Loves* (1979). The novel combines academic satire with a nonsatiric portrait of the artist, Brigit Stott, as a 39-year-old divorcée, novelist, and university teacher. Because Oates has not before portrayed in a novel an intellectual woman committed to professional work, or explored in a novel what is surely the passionate center of her own existence, literature and writing, this work seems to represent a welcome lowering of defenses, allowing her to draw more directly from her immediate experience. Moreover, some facets of Brigit's experience recall earlier Oatesian portraits of women: Elena in *Do With Me What You Will* and Laney in *Childwold*. Brigit also looks forward to later women: Monica and Sheila in *Solstice* and Marya in *Marya: A Life*.

Looking at these women together, one can see an important evolutionary development across Oates's canon in her portrayals of the potentialities of female selfhood. *Unholy Loves* is an uncharacteristically affirmative work, recording Brigit's breakthrough into autonomy, maturity, and artistic commitment, effected in large part through her curious relationship with an elderly English poet, Albert St. Dennis, who is brought in as Distinguished Professor of Poetry at her college, Woodslee, for the year.

As God is at the center of *Son in the Morning*, the object of Nathanael's delusional "holy love," St. Dennis is at the center of *Unholy Loves*. Considered to be the best living poet—second only to Yeats in this century—he is the frail vessel of the hopes and aspirations of the many Woodslee academics who court his favor. Brigit had fantasized before his arrival that she would fall in love with him, they would marry, and the burden of her unfulfilled life and failure as a novelist would drop away. She soon sees that he is simply too old to be one of her Augustinian "unholy loves" (The title comes from a passage in St. Augustine's *Confessions,* quoted in the novel: "To Carthage then I came, where a cauldron of unholy loves sang all about mine ears").[9] St. Dennis becomes instead a "holy love," inspiring both profane and sacred passions within her.

Through St. Dennis's presumption that Brigit and Alexis Kessler, a colleague from the music department, are lovers, they do in fact become lovers. In the profuse Yeatsian echoes that infuse the work, they receive the blessing of this "aged man" who is "but a paltry thing" and become "the young in one another's arms," caught up in "sensual music." Brigit's relationship with Alexis is part of her maturation as a woman and as an artist. The liberating quality of this union is uncritically treated: it pulls Brigit out of a deep "despair, utter blankness of the soul" (*UL*, 25). Its compulsive passions are driving and undeniable, opening Brigit up to liberating sexuality, although the language used to describe their lovemaking could hardly be described as lyrical:

Bucking, heaving, straining. Her heartbeat ferocious. She grasps at him, clutches at him. . . . With Alexis she is open and helpless and raw and heaving and it frightens her to know she must seem ugly to him, her mouth gaping, her eyes dilated, but she cannot stop, she does not want to stop, he embraces her tightly as if unaware of her terror. She is about to lose control of herself. . . . She is terrified of losing control of herself; she is terrified that she will not lose control but will remain behind, unchanged. . . . A horrible childlike wailing—she hears it, it fills the room, it cannot be disowned (*UL*, 130–31, 134).

The Lawrencean baptism of fire in passion, the coming to fuller selfhood by losing control of the conscious self is a common Oatesian theme. Brigit, like Elena in *Do With Me What You Will*, develops through this union an increased ability to take hold of her own life.

Yet while the relationship with Alexis is fulfilling for a time, Brigit abruptly and violently ends it. Eventually, she "outlive[s] that desire, in a way she . . . triumph[s] over it" (*UL*, 310), and she sublimates its passionate energy in her art—a transformation that is perhaps essential to the creation of art. Reflecting on "Leda and the Swan," St. Dennis thinks, "*That*, is the secret, perhaps, behind all art: the violent use of the flesh, of any flesh, and then its abandonment" (*UL*, 16). Furthermore, Brigit is at a stage in her life—midlife transition—that Oates has noted as being of particular significance for herself and many other people, not incidentally including 33-year-old St. Augustine, whose midlife conversion from unholy to holy love is alluded to in the title.

Among other adjustments, Brigit has to come to terms with herself as a no-longer-young woman who will now seldom if ever again turn heads as does another character, Sandra Jaeger; a person for whom, it is implied, sexuality is less important than it once was. Alexis, younger than she and bisexual as well, is still caught in "sensual music," still reaching for an elusive harmony through sexual union: "they are a relationship, a slightly discordant harmony. He *hears* them but cannot see them. Cannot touch them. It is not her body he wants but it is only through the body that he can take possession of another human being . . . There is no way into the soul of another except through the body, Alexis thinks, saddened" (*UL*, 333).

But Brigit hears different music in the voice of the singing-master of her soul, St. Dennis. Indeed, Brigit sometimes confuses her "lovers": "It is Alexis she loves, it is St. Dennis she loves" (*UL*, 107). Despite St. Dennis's frequent drunkenness and incipient senility, and although he feels himself to be "expected to perform, monkey-like, dancing-bear-like, chattering-parrot-like" (*UL*, 6), there is no discrediting his achievement; his poetry has movingly transmuted private experience into "monuments of unaging intellect." He has "created himself" through his work: "Alone among men the poet creates himself. As Yeats knew. Through the strenuous activity of his art. Through the cruel, heart-straining pilgrimage of his art. He risks despair and madness and exclusion from life's feast in order to create his own soul. Alone among men" (*UL*, 7). Through his consciousness is expressed the pains ("torture, the refinement of emotion into art") and the delights of artistic creation: "Anonymity of art when one surrenders entirely to it, delicious privacy of perfection, inexpressible joy. He does not dare hope that anyone else can understand" (*UL*, 105).

Not only is his "voice" an inspiration to Brigit; his shocking death in an apartment fire (again echoing Yeats: "O sages standing in God's holy fire . . .") reawakens other voices demanding expression—those of her grandfather and other relatives callously dismissed long ago. Now she experiences grief for her grandparents' deaths, too, as she had not as a girl. In the emotion that washes over her, she begins to write about her family and early years with new energy, absorption, and self-forgetfulness: "It was upsetting, it was draining, it demanded her entire attention, yet she rather enjoyed it—she could not remember, in fact having enjoyed anything quite so much" (*UL*, 307).

Brigit feels as well the tempting pull of another world—the world of the unconscious, a looking-glass world. Like Alice in Wonderland, she is tempted to step into this mysteriously, spiritually vibrant and interconnected other world, yet it is dangerous; visions and images would invade her being, and her ego would be threatened with extinction:

In recent weeks she had been thinking [of] . . . the world of her dream, through the mirror, across the threshold, into a realm of ghost-images, ghost-selves, utter mystery. She had been subject to sudden, piercing memories, almost entirely visual, that come to her with the force of cards being held up before her eyes. She cannot see. She cannot resist. . . . She is *Brigit* but there is some danger . . . there is some danger of her losing *Brigit* if she does not turn back . . . Suddenly the world about her is alive. The world, the universe: a gigantic living creature. . . . She is fearful of that other world, she does not want to cross into it, she knows very well that it exists, simultaneous with this world; but she is not ready for it yet. Not yet. (*UL*, 312–13)

This passage, I suspect, is heavily autobiographical, depicting Oates's own visionary dreams—her receptivity to powerful images, emotions, and forces that come from outside of the conscious self. It recalls passages in *Childwold* and anticipates not only the play on light and dark consciousness in *Solstice* but also Marya Knauer's apprehension, in *Marya: A Life,* of the disturbing, self-annihilating potential of a visionary other world. Oates herself, of course, claims to draw inspiration from both the day and night sides of consciousness. Brigit "is not ready" for those darker illuminations, "not yet."

In her passionate commitment to transcribing her remembered childhood, however, Brigit experiences a new calm. Rather than being locked in a staid academic world and an unliberated self, she feels an opening up to possibilities at the end of the novel: "whatever happens to me for the rest of my life . . . won't be inevitable. I think that is why I feel so optimistic." Alexis questions this optimism: "But surely, my love, that can't last?" (*UL*, 335). Perhaps not, but her willingness to face whatever may come seems positive and recalls the joyful acceptance of risks by the liberated Elena in *Do With Me What You Will,* and contrasts sharply with Nathanael's empty waiting at the end of *Son of the Morning.*

Unholy Loves is about balance: about the successful negotiation of the conscious and the unconscious self, about the transmutation of art out of life. It demonstrates, I think, Oates's essentially romantic and modernist artistic allegiances. Art grows out of the "white heat" of the unconscious; it requires a romantic opening up to "the unconscious, the oceanic, ungovernable, unfathomable reservoir of human energy," but such experiences must be balanced with a craftsmanlike "intelligence and discretion and transcendence."[10] Art grows out of life, but it can transcend it: through their works artists can create themselves anew; the artist's work can survive mutability. Oates suggests both in this novel and in critical essays such as "The Dream of the 'Sacred Text.'"

This portrait of the artist is, however, yoked with academic satire. While Oates takes the artist seriously, she is caustically critical of Brigit's academic residence, the shallow, partygoing world of Woodslee University, a respected, well-endowed private university in upper New York State. The novel echoes Oates's earlier short story collection *The Hungry Ghosts* (1974) as it mercilessly lays bare academic lives contorted and thwarted by rampant ambition, personal vendettas, inflated and bruised egos, backbiting and apocryphal gossip, sexual opportunism, misguided scholarship, hysterical emptiness, self-absorbed insensitivity, elitism, and cliquishness. Indeed, the novel is structured around a series of parties that only serve to highlight the shallowness and pettiness of the academic social masquerade.

Brigit Stott speculates on the "indifferent performance" of the "social persona," in contrast to "the rich and deep and strange and inexplicable" interior life:

Brigit had noted even as a young girl the curious fact that while "real" people often presented themselves as shallow and not very likeable, "fictional" characters of a high order revealed themselves as marvelously complex, no less devious and subtle than Brigit believed herself to be. Her external self, her social persona, *Brigit Stott,* hardly represented her—it was, in fact, an indifferent performance at best, since her imagination was usually elsewhere; and she assumed that the same was true of everyone. The interior life is rich and deep and strange and inexplicable, and the exterior life—the "social" life—is no more complex than it needs to be. *Brigit Stott* is a character she lavishes little skill on: it is a vessel, a means, a transparency. (*UL,* 260)

While Oates herself has made similar comments about the relative value of the interior life (as have her characters, such as John Fitz Kasch and Laney in *Childwold*), one cannot help but feel that the host of characters who populate this novel are "no more complex" than they need to be. Only Brigit is accorded full stature as a complex and sympathetic human being. The others receive very little nourishment from the intellectual community Alexis says he craves, or fulfillment from teaching and scholarship, or enrichment from the large part of experience presumably lived outside of the consuming passions of academe. Even Woodslee's most impeccable scholar, Gowan Vaughan-Jones, whose private life is totally (and somewhat ludicrously) submerged in his work, is apparently incapable of understanding St. Dennis as another artist, Brigit, knows he truly was. Gowan's scholarship is an "invention" ("it is not the poet St. Dennis of whom Gowan speaks so much as his own invention, a masterful 'satirist' of the first rank, and it is certainly not the man St. Dennis of whom he speaks—not the man Brigit knew"), and Gowan's life is parasitic: "*here,* among the world's population, is the individual who will most benefit from St. Dennis's life and death" (*UL,* 319).

These exaggerated characters limit the resonance of the work. So too does the novel's style lack grace; there is too much piling up of detail about boring parties and boring people. Nonetheless, what sustains *Unholy Loves* is its sensitive portrait of a woman novelist who is made tranquil and whole through the "holy love" of art.

Cybele

Where God, emblem of divinity, is the love object at the center of *Son of the Morning,* and St. Dennis, emblem of art, is at the center of *Unholy Loves,* Cybele, emblem of erotic desire, is at the center of *Cybele* (1979). This book too is about the quest for transcendence through love. Like *Unholy Loves,* this novel is highly allusive and satiric; unlike *Unholy Loves,* no redemption is posited. Treated distantly and sardonically, Edwin Locke, the questing central character, is dead when the novel begins. The book is a retrospective portrait of him, told—at least intermittently—from the point of view of an unnamed, dispassionate mistress, undoubtedly the Cybele of the book's title.

Oates is fascinated by the Great Mother in her mythic embodiments as Kali or Cybele and in her modern-day manifestations as the strong, passionate, selfish, self-confident, demanding "mothers" in her canon, who intimidate their often fragile daughters while inspiring passionate adulation from men. Foregrounded in the novel is not the myth but the modern-day story of Edwin Locke, insurance executive bored with his marriage, who "discovers" real life and love through a series of affairs—starting with Cathleen Diehl, the wife in one of the couples in their circle of friends.

Like other of Oates's books, *Cybele* traces the hallucinogenic, obsessive, and slightly absurd condition of being "in love"—the overwhelming sense of promise for self-authentication: "He realizes that he is, after a lifetime of illusion, about to break free . . . about to discover himself. A frightening process. Terrifying. But necessary. To *know* himself to *be*."[11] But, unlike some of her portrayals of erotic love, including the relationship of Brigit and Alexis in *Unholy Loves,* this one is unequivocally antiromantic. It is indeed a burlesque of romance, depicting the inevitable eroding of desire, the self-delusion it involves, and the need for ever-more-base stimuli.[12] After his affections for Cathleen Diehl wane, Edwin goes to Risa Allen—of a lower social class, more earthy, more vulgar, more self-assured. With her Edwin feels that he is on the brink of transcendence of inauthenticity ("*One of the most profound moments of my life. When truth at last asserted itself*" [C, 87]). But the language of the text is increasingly laden with the irony of Edwin's self-deluding obsession: "To awake! To live! To plunge forward bravely, even recklessly, into the life that was meant for him all along: *this is why we are born,* Edwin Locke thinks, as he turns onto Sussex Lane" (*C,* 98).

Sussex Lane is where he lives his married life. His confession of his relationship with Risa precipitates a "Great Quarrel" with his wife, Cynthia, and their eventual separation, after which there is a comically well-realized attempt at reconciliation. The joke is on the reader in a way, for the novel records an encounter between Edwin and an unidentified woman in a bar. He is boldly forward, commenting suggestively upon her sensuality and eventually inviting her to his hotel room, which he describes as the honeymoon suite complete with Spanish flamenco music and erotic films. But when he can't find the key, the drama is broken. The stranger turns out to be Cynthia, who in wifely fashion complains about Edwin's poor performance: "Tonight of all nights. Deliberately. And you're drunk, aren't you. You were drinking before you met me. And you saw to it that I'm drunk. Didn't you. And that tie—the dry cleaners never got that gravy stain out of it, can't you see?—can't you for God's sake *see?* I thought I'd thrown that thing out years ago but somehow you still *have* it, you must have hoarded it. . . ." She begins to cry, her shoulders shaking, her face distorted. "Tonight of all nights. Oh Edwin, *tonight of all nights*" (*C,* 122).

The encounter, we find out later, was suggested by a Dr. Gidding, marital therapist, to instill new romance into a tired marriage. The experience goes from bad to worse as Edwin, in the hotel room, tries to stir up his sexual interest by rubbing oil on the lardy flesh of his wife; all he can do is look despairingly at his watch and try to endure the experience. His mind wanders helplessly until finally, irresistibly, he thinks of squid and breaks into hysterical laughter. With Cynthia outraged and insulted, Edwin "rolls onto the floor, half-sobbing, his oily body picking up lint and dust from the carpet" (*C,* 140).

This fiasco cements their separation. Edwin is soon onto his relationship with Iris, a masseuse, and then with her housemate, Zanche, the probable Cybele of the book's title (although I think Oates's point is that all of the women are various manifestations of herself). With Zanche, though, the mythologic symbolism is playfully alluded to, both in the general theme of the narrative and in some of its details.

Cybele is the mother goddess of fertility, made infamous in Catullus's poem about Attis, a man maddened to the point of castrating himself in frenzied worship of her—an act he later regrets. The novel is riddled with playful implicit parallels to the myths surrounding this Great Mother, especially concerning the dangers of uncritical worship. "Bold clever deft daring impatient passionate Zanche, the most extraordinary woman Edwin Locke ever knew" (*C,* 171), inspires in him a delirious adulation. He achieves with her sexual fulfillment to belie the impotence and boredom he experiences with his wife. But Zanche, like the other magna maters who haunt Oates's pages, is a destroyer of masculinity as well as an object of attraction. Foulmouthed, self-centered, unfaithful, indifferent, Zanche keeps the flames of another romance going with an earlier lover, Valentin Rok. Increasingly sensualized and degraded in his need for erotic stimulation, Edwin longs to be an observer of Zanche and Rok's lovemaking. Finally, he sinks to an attempted rape of Zanche's nine-year-old retarded daughter, but he discovers to his horror that she is a hermaphrodite. Sickened and enraged, he lashes out violently at Zanche's apartment just as she and Rok come in. In Rok's pursuit of him, Edwin is apparently both castrated and stricken with a fatal heart attack.

Oates's modern-day Cybele, the supremely self-confident narrator, is convinced that Edwin Locke "worshipped her" and at the very moment of

his death "was thinking of [her]" (*C*, 15). Indeed, in a strange passage near
the end of the novel, Edwin is said to be daydreaming of an immense hill
within which he wants to burrow, a mountain that becomes the womanly
flesh within which he is finally trapped:

An immense hill into which he wants to burrow. Head-first. Trembling with desire.
Sobbing with desire. And the hill becomes flesh, and the flesh seems to flinch from
his violence, his need, whimpering as if it were alive; but still he forces himself into
it. Like this! Like this! Like this! And as he forces himself into it, it does give way, it
succumbs, he pounds at it with his head, plunging, burrowing, half-choking with
the rage of his desire, until he has penetrated my very core. Like this! he cries. Oh
God like this!
     And then the flesh, which has parted for him, in fear of him, begins to contract.
     And, horribly, he is caught in me. Trapped.
     Swallowed alive!
     He screams for help, for release. But of course no one hears. His screams are not
audible, nor is there anyone to hear. For I have him fast, and tight, in the hot tight
blood-thrumming depths of me, and he will never withdraw, no matter how franti-
cally he struggles to get free, no matter how valiantly his poor strained heart beats: I
have him, I have him forever. (*C*, 193–94)

Cybele, the goddess of the mountains, is here made encasing flesh—a gross
fantasy, the ultimate extension of the male fear of the engulfing female. Indeed, the black stone that Edwin gives Zanche as a gift is another reminder
of the goddess, who was said to have been embodied in the small black me-
teorite that the Romans delivered to Rome and enshrined in the Palatine hill
to help them to victory in the Hannibalic War in 204 B.C. Similarly,
Zanche's lover Valentin Rok is another symbol of the rock and of the "love"
goddess herself: he effects the castration and death of her worshipper. Edwin
is unmanned both figuratively and literally by Rok's knife. Also, the ambiguous sexual identity of Zanche's daughter is a reminder of the forfeited
sexuality of Cybele's eunuch servers. And the "female" acquaintance of
Zanche who flirts with Edwin and then reveals herself to be a man has cym-
bals, which recall the instrument associated with the festivals of Cybele.[13]
     Oates playfully, and I think successfully, weaves allusions to these ancient
myths throughout her modern story. The story succeeds on a realistic level,
but it is enriched by its mythologic extensions. The frenzied adulation of
Cybele, the self-mutilation and the wild and violent orgies, were anoma-
lous, "foreign" importations into the sober, orderly, and dignified world of
the Romans. Yet this worship apparently ministered to some deep-seated
emotional need in the populace, at least for a time. So too is Edwin Locke's

passionate obsession with Zanche both an aberration from his normal middle-class life and an expression of emotional need. Oates is very attuned to the obsession of such libidinal drives. The tone of the novel, of course, is mocking, distanced, and comic. We shed no tears over Edwin's fate. Oates, like other moderns attracted to the Cybele-Attis story,[14] cannot resist the comic dimensions of frenzied, emasculating worship of the magna mater. Edwin, like Attis, loses his dignity as well as his masculinity and his life through this obsession. The novel will never be considered one of Oates's best works, but it is an interesting example of how she writes within a rich tradition of literary antecedents. Oates does not seem to experience an anxiety of influence. Rather, she readily acknowledges her literary borrowings—here, in the very title of the novel—and uses allusion with playful invention.

Angel of Light

Angel of Light (1981), another novel rich in literary allusion, is built upon an implicit parallel to Aeschylus's *Oresteia*. The story concerns the avenging of the death of Maurice (Maurie) Halleck, director of the Commission for the Ministry of Justice, by his children, Owen and Kirsten. Accused of wrongdoing, Maurie has died in a car crash—a seeming suicide. But like Orestes and Electra, his children believe that his death is the result of a plot by their mother, Isabel. In their eyes, she and her lover, Nick Martens, are as guilty of murder as were Clytemnestra and Aegisthus. At the beginning of the book Kirsten and Owen make a pact to avenge their father's death.

The novel moves forward from March 1980, when Owen and Kirsten make their revenge pact, through the successive months of plotting until September 1980, when Owen murders his mother and Kirsten seriously injures Nick Martens. Alternating chapters retrospectively fill in the past, focusing particularly on the special friendship between Maurie and Nick, which began when they were boys at boarding school and continued through their adulthood—a relationship complicated by Nick's clandestine adulterous liaison with Isabel.

Oates said in an interview that she began writing *Angel of Light* in 1959; this makes it one of her earliest novels.[15] She put it aside and didn't take it up again until 1981. This unusual genesis explains why the novel is reminiscent of earlier works and quite unlike the fabulistic novels (*Bellefleur* and *A Bloodsmoor Romance*) that immediately preceded and followed its publication. While the novel was started in the fifties, its climate is reminiscent of the sixties, echoing Watergate, the Symbionese Liberation Army, political misdeeds, and a politicized youth culture dedicated to the purification of a corrupt order.

Like the other novels considered in this chapter, *Angel of Light* is about love. At the center of this novel is the enigmatic love object Maurie Halleck. He is the cause of his children's revenge pact; his idealistic quest for goodness and his commitment to loyalty, love, and justice contrast with the baser motivations of his wife and her lover; his Christlike self-sacrifice for them has a devastating and perhaps cathartic effect.

This novel is, in a way, another version of *The Assassins*. Both books are about the effect of the suicide of a central political figure on his immediate family. In both books an intense brotherly relationship (in *The Assassins*, that of Andrew and Stephen Petrie; here, of Maurie and Nick) dramatizes dualities of being.

The special bond between Maurie and Nick goes back to a boyhood incident in which Nick saved Maurie from drowning in a water-rafting accident. Maurie feels a debt of gratitude to Nick, a boy he admires and who is in many ways his opposite. Wealthy and well connected, Maurie is slight, small, and homely, "with his gnomish monkeyish face," good-hearted, embarrassing in his talk of God and Christ and the privilege of being alive. In contrast, Nick, of much less wealthy origins, is popular, a leader, handsome, self-assured, athletic, talented, brimming with ambition and self-absorption. Yet the two develop into good friends, almost brothers: "Maurie was his good conscience, perhaps. His younger brother." They would talk and argue late at night "about religion and what it means to be religious: to *be* a form of Christ." Maurie claims to be "waiting" for a religious experience.[16]

The difference between the two is effectively dramatized in the scene in which they meet at boarding school. Maurie is the first to arrive at the suite of rooms they are to share. When Nick appears Maurie explains that he "ha[s] taken the bedroom on the left because it face[s] the courtyard and might get the most noise in the morning. And he ha[s] taken the smallest bookshelf." Nick, after coolly sizing him up, proclaims that Maurie had taken the room because it faces the south, has the best light, has a good view, and is the largest room: but that was his privilege because he was the first there. Maurie "beg[s] and explain[s] and apologize[s]" and insists that Nick take the room. Finally, Nick takes the room in triumph, with a certain disdain for his fawning suite mate (*AL*, 61–62). Maurie's desire to be good and Nick's to win characterize them throughout the novel. Maurie is an idealistic dreamer, Nick a Faustian schemer; one seeks higher sanctification, the other success in this world.

Maurie assists his friend in his career. Nick becomes the associate director of the Commission of the Ministry of Justice. Later, after Maurie's death, he takes over as director. Much earlier, he takes over Maurie's beautiful wife, Isabel. From the first moment of meeting, Nick and Isabel are strongly attracted to one another. Urged by Maurie to become friends, they go for a walk on the beach that ends in a romantic liaison. Their infatuation with one another continues over 20 years, although Maurie is not explicitly confronted with it until near the end, when Isabel asks him for a separation during a devastating disclosure: "I've had lovers, Isabel hears herself telling Maurie, I've been in love, she tells him, but not in a sobbing 'confessional' voice, for Isabel is too cultivated for such drivel, please don't be upset Maurie but I've been in love and I know what I'm capable of as a woman and—forgive me—it was always a pretense, with you: and I think you knew" (*AL*, 347). Maurie did not know, and the revelation is a blow that contributes to his choice of death.

Isabel's betrayal is coupled by Nick's. Evidence begins to mount that something is wrong in the Ministry of Justice. When Maurie asks Nick about it, he denies any knowledge—a bold and obvious lie, since Nick has been criminally involved in collusion, cover-up, and bribery in a commission investigation. After Maurie's death, Nick is obsessed with trying to plead his own case to his lost friend:

I gave in because I had come to feel that we didn't really have enough evidence anyway—it was all so circumstantial, the witnesses were so unreliable—and the regime had been gone so long, so very long—everyone dead—Allende forgotten—and now there's Guatemala—and tomorrow there will be another scandal: United Fruit, Gulf and Western, Lockheed, GBT Copper: which is which, and why, and when, and how can it possibly matter? To accept so-called monies in order to retard an investigation that was doomed in any case, to sabotage a prosecution that didn't require sabotage to look insubstantial in front of a shrewd judge . . . it appealed to my sense of humor (*AL*, 391).

Moral and upright, Maurie would never have understood or participated in such an action, yet he confesses to exactly that. Before his suicide, Maurie admits to having committed numerous misdeeds at the Commission: acceptance of bribery, stalling of prosecution, sabotage of documents. His confessed guilt is in fact that of Nick. He deliberately sacrifices himself out of love for Nick and Isabel: "To humble oneself, to empty oneself—even of goodness. Christ's final sacrifice: the sacrifice of divinity itself" (*AL*, 363).

The Hallecks are distant descendants of John Brown, who took comfort in the fact that "*I am permitted* to die for a cause and not merely to pay the debt of nature as all must" (*AL,* 12). Brown was called by Thoreau an "*Angel of Light.*" Thoreau said: "*I do not wish to kill or be killed but I can foresee circumstances in which both of these things would be by me unavoidable*" (*AL,* 14). So too, it is implied, does Maurie die for a cause: "Maurie's fingers close about the keys. His heart swells with sudden gratitude—wave upon wave of calm—peace—lucidity—certainty. I die to clear the way for others. I die to erase shame. To shock them into the purity of soul of which they have always been capable" (*AL,* 360).

Initially, Isabel and Nick do not appear to be capable of this purity of soul. At the beginning of the novel, some nine months after Maurie's death, Isabel has fully resumed her busy, self-absorbed social life. She is a very popular Washington personality whose activities are reported regularly in the society pages. She continues to have various lovers in addition to Nick. So too does Nick's career prosper: he is sworn in as the Director of the Commission for the Ministry of Justice, Maurie's old position. Yet late in the novel we have some indication of the chilling effect Maurie's death has on the lovers. Isabel feels their responsibility and predicts their ultimate punishment: "We did it, Isabel is whispering, we killed him, we'll be punished, but Nick makes another attempt to hold her as if he hasn't heard. . . . Isabel says angrily: You killed him that day you lied to him—it's as simple as that. . . . So he's dead, Isabel says, and for what?—everything is over. We'll be punished. No one knows, Nick says angrily, we *can't* be punished. He should have let you go to jail, Isabel says. He should have prepared the case himself.—No, it's all over. I hate us. We will be punished" (*AL,* 385–86).

While Nick is very pleased with the success of his career, he is always aware of the lies and deception upon which his success rests. It occurs to him as he reads one flattering piece about himself that the person being described "isn't Nick Martens . . . but Maurie Halleck. Idealistic, apolitical, contemptuous of party politics. Committed to his work. To his profession. Incorruptible. And feared—as a consequence of his very incorruptibility" (*AL,* 391). A certain indifference sets in: "since Maurie's death very little matters. For the universe has shifted—subtly but irreparably. Very little matters: what Nick does, or what is done to him" (*AL,* 393). Like other characters in close relationships in Oates's fiction, Nick and Maurie seem to need each other for a sense of completeness, recalling Stephen and Andrew Petrie in *The Assassins.* When Maurie is gone, Nick is adrift.

Kirsten and Owen—the modern-day Electra and Orestes, respectively— feel they must kill their mother and her lover, both to avenge their mother's killing of their father and to restore justice to the world. Oates dedicates the book to classics scholar Robert Fagles "in honor of his service in the House of Atreus; and for our lost generations." Kirsten is indeed "lost" at the beginning of the novel. This once-beautiful girl, now anorexic, filthy, unpopular, and unpleasant, broods over the culpability of her mother. In contrast, Owen, four years older, "is gentlemanly and easily embarrassed and reliable and intelligent and ambitious and canny, the very best (so he fears) of second-best" (*AL*, 26).

Yet Owen becomes as obsessed as his sister. He gets involved with a revolutionary group called the Doves, who are supposedly dedicated to peace but who are planning various violent events to accelerate the "evolution of revolutionary consciousness on all class levels." They "declare PERPETUAL WAR upon the Fascist Capitalist Class and all their employees, agents, sycophants, and dupes. We do hereby declare ourselves SELF-EMPOWERED under the RIGHTS OF MAN" (*AL*, 370–71). Owen believes "that after the mission is completed—his mission, and Kirsten's—he will enter a new phase of his life, a 'radically altered vision,' in Ulrich May's words. Both he and Kirsten. Baptized in blood. 'Crossing over'" (*AL*, 373).

When Owen performs the grisly act of killing his mother, he brings along some of the revolutionary propaganda, but he is in fact little interested in it. His motivation is not really political at all; it is as personal as Kirsten's. After the matricide Owen is overcome with fatigue. In a scene dripping with Freudian associations, he reverts to a childlike state, rocking back and forth with his thumb in his mouth, recalling his childhood cradle. He lies down for a brief rest on his mother's bed and falls asleep, dreaming of his mother rubbing gently against his cheek. He is sound asleep when the bomb he had earlier planted blows up the house. Like Richard Everett's alleged matricide in *Expensive People*, Owen's killing of his mother is a way of fixing son and mother forever in the Oedipal bond. With the offending adult mother destroyed, Owen recreates momentarily the loving mother of his childhood and then, seeking union with her, unconsciously chooses his own death as he sinks into sleep. Oates has again and again dramatized variations on this claustrophobic and destructive family romance.

Meanwhile, Kirsten lures Nick Martens into a seeming romantic rendezvous. In avenging her father by taking over her mother's lover, she too is working through complicated oedipal bonds. She attempts to stab Nick to death, but she is not strong enough to deal a deathly blow. He lives on, bleeding into the mattress. Finally, she anonymously calls the police, and Nick is saved. Kirsten disappears from town; she is said to be living with relatives in Minneapolis.

At the end of the novel, in a section called "Exiles," Nick is depicted as a recluse, living inconspicuously on the beach and writing unanswered letters to Kirsten. After the attempt on his life, he had confessed to his complicity at the Commission and resigned his job. He protects Kirsten's identity and her role in the attack. Nick feels that he has in fact died and writes of what happens to him after his death. In the novel's inconclusive ending, he accepts their separate exiles and is left empty of expectation.

Nick, the lone survivor with an aimless existence, is reminiscent of other Oates characters: Stephen Petrie in *The Assassins,* Kasch in *Childwold,* and Nathanael in *Son of the Morning.* I suppose one can see the change in Nick as growth: he confesses, he forgives, he attempts reconciliation, but he is a broken man, cut off from involvement in the world.

Indeed, while *Angel of Light* is allegedly a novel about politics and our political heritage, it is predominantly about the private lives of individuals, with only tenuous connections to issues that reach beyond the personal. Maurie and Nick's professional lives at the Commission for the Ministry of Justice are very sketchily summarized, not at all dramatized. One can only piece together in a fragmentary fashion what political issues underlie the action. We know generally that Maurie is principled and honest and that Nick is opportunistic and dishonest, but we don't see how those traits are manifested in the political arena. For much of the book we are as confused as the other characters about Maurie's confession of guilt.

Also contributing to the book's hazy political context is the stereotypical treatment of the revolutionary group Owen joins. Owen has only the vaguest sense of what they are about, and the reader must share his limited vision. In a five-page paragraph Oates summarizes the manner in which Owen records the heavy rhetoric and actions of this group:

He is often missing names now, parts of sentences, connective tissue in debates that wind on and on through the night, like tinsel-ribbon, glittering and blinding. . . . We are continually at war, it is continual wartime in this country, though at heart we are at peace . . . we are repulsed by violence . . . even necessary violence. The Doves. The Silver Doves. Named for a legendary secret sect . . . Russia . . . pre-Revolutionary Russia. Buddy and Rita Stone and Adrienne and Shirley and Smitty and Brock. Amos, a week's stay. Sam, coming up from Miami, who never arrives after a succession of late-night telephone calls. . . . Taxi drivers, parking garage attendants, a part-time instructor (remedial English) at American University. . . . We call ourselves the Doves because in our hearts we are peaceful and peace is the only hope of the world. In our essence there is no contention but a oneness, a unity, a symbiosis of all warring elements. . . . Plans for a fall offensive. To coincide with. To underscore. To dramatize. To awaken. Current social crises are accelerating the evolution of revolutionary consciousness on all class levels . . . not just among the workers and disenfranchised students. Scandals, corruption, hired government assassins. The candidacy of Reagan. Fascist-reactionary powers consolidating. Imminent police state. Takeover. Military. Educational institutions shut down. Censorship. Summary executions. War." (*AL*, 369)

A satiric and unsympathetic portrait, to be sure, but the language is very nearly unreadable.

Owen and Kirsten do not convincingly assume the roles of Orestes and Electra in seeking to avenge their father's death. They are neither attractive nor vividly rendered, although Oates piles up a tremendous amount of descriptive detail in portraying them, particularly Kirsten. As a result, the text has a staccato, breathless quality and gives the reader too much unassimilated information to process:

An introvert, a loner, passive-aggressive, bright, quick, inventive, unsocial, remarkable facility for language, troublemaker, ringleader, sarcastic, naturally good-humored, witty, funny, comedian, clown, in fact voted class clown at Hayes, her second and final year at that prestigious school, depressive personality, manic interludes, prone to fantasizing, high I.Q., wide range of interests, unusual maturity, sympathy for overseas orphans, project on Vietnamese children, project on John Brown, perfectionist, impatient, immature, sloppy work habits, inability to listen to authority, unfunny in fact potentially dangerous sense of humor. . . . Insomniac, anorexic, gay and chattering nonstop, mute for days, not showering, not changing clothes, rude to her roommate, weeping in her roommate's arms, sending Owen that repulsive message. . . . That small white grim insufferable face. Starving herself. Fainting in gym class and on the stairs. Silent in class, her arms folded tight across her breasts. Staring. Smirking. Faint lines on her forehead. An odor of inconsolable grief, stale as unwashed clothes. Alone and stubborn and light-headed. (*AL*, 30–31, 32, 37)

Moreover, we don't know what effect Kirsten's attempted murder of Nick has had on her: she fades out of the novel. Owen, of course, is dead, and one can feel no grief; throughout, he is an unappealing character, confused in motivation.

The most interesting characters of the book are Isabel and Nick, and the most successfully rendered scenes are those involving them. Isabel is yet another version of the strong, predatory "mothers" who populate Oates's fiction, intimidating their anorexic daughters. Reminiscent of Clara, Loretta, Nada, Ardis, Arlene, and others, Isabel de Benavente Halleck is perhaps the most beautiful and polished of the lot, and certainly the most successful:

She "was one of the three or four highest-ranking Washington hostesses of
the era" (*AL*, 131). In the characteristic style of the book, Oates lists the
"many and varied" guests "who are to pass through Isabel Halleck's salon in
the handsome stone house at 18 Rocken, in her foreshortened but brilliant
career as a Washington hostess": they range from prime ministers, shahs,
premiers, presidents, and kings to famous athletes, musicians, university
professors, rock singers, feminists, and financiers. Isabel is a very human
character, selfish and egotistical yet with moments of warmth, self-criticism,
and humor.

So too is Nick convincingly portrayed in the round. He is a self-made,
passionate man in the grips of a powerful ambition and a powerful attraction to Isabel. As much as Maurie denies his own gratification, Nick in-
dulges "his ambition, his old lust. His tireless plotting. Nick Martens as he
knows and values himself. Nick Martens as the world observes him, pious
with envy.—Let me exist, to begin with, Nick has often wanted to say, to
shout, in angry justification of himself: let me for Christ's sake *exist* and the
rest of the world can fall in place around me" (*AL*, 389). He is reminiscent
of Andrew Petrie in *The Assassins* in his attempt to impose a powerful will
on reality.

Angel of Light is reminiscent in many ways of other Oates works that de-
pict patterns of claustrophobic and obsessive family romance: grisly matricide, which is also a regressive longing for oneness with the mother;
powerful mother and weak daughter engaged in complex oedipal relationships with father/husband and lover; "brothers" locked in powerful rivalry
and love, one playing out the ego's drives, the other yearning for selfless
oneness with God or goodness, one taking over the life (and wife) of the
other, the death of one leaving the other bereft and confused.

In this book as in others, family romance is also the external manifestation of psychic drama. That these recurrent patterns of behavior have
ancient antecedents adds to their credibility and resonance. But the sociological extension—the attempt to set this drama within the larger context of
corrupt Washingtonian politics and counterculture movements—is less successful. And the novel is marred by its unhoned style, particularly its unre-
strained piling up of facts and descriptive phrases.

But the book is an interesting addition to the dialogue on love and the
possibilities of transcendence through love. In *Son of the Morning*
Nathanael's quest for oneness with God ultimately becomes an egotistical
delusion that he *is* God and an intolerance of the human world. In *Angel of
Light* Maurie's idealism, his quest for goodness, is different: it is neither
egotistical nor otherworldly. Although he is in some ways an unlikely

hero—a foolish and deluded man betrayed by his wife and friend—his steadfast commitment to love, loyalty, justice, and goodness does make him, in some ways, a modern-day "angel of light." These qualities do not redeem him or others, perhaps, but they do raise life above the basest level and reflect an important strain of idealism in the American character. Oates's novels are often fundamentally about the American dream, the quest for something higher, better, the chance to create oneself and one's society anew. In this novel, Nick Martens, the character most driven to realize for himself the American dream, shows its corruptibility when driving personal ambition is unleavened by idealism or altruism. The self-sacrificial death of his alter ego, Maurie, does at least cause him to see the emptiness and delusion of his quest.

Angel of Light is not a particularly hopeful novel, however. The "justice" sought by Kirsten and Owen is deeply confused and embedded in arrested libidinal development. Their essential aimlessness makes them easy dupes for the misguided idealism of absurd revolutionary groups. A much more optimistic book, as well as a much more imaginative playing out of the dualities at the heart of the American dream and the American character, is the novel published the year before this one, *Bellefleur.*

Chapter Three
Genres Reenvisioned

Nothing Oates had written before quite anticipated the boldly experimental, parodic *Bellefleur* (1980) or the subsequent novels in a similar vein, *A Bloodsmoor Romance* (1982) and *Mysteries of Winterthurn* (1984). Along with a fourth volume,[1] which has been listed as forthcoming for some time, these novels, Oates says, are designed as "as a quartet of experimental novels that deal, in genre form, with nineteenth-century and early twentieth-century America": the family saga in *Bellefleur,* the domestic romance in *Bloodsmoor Romance,* the detective thriller in *Mysteries of Winterthurn,* and the forthcoming "Gothic horror set in turn-of-the-century Princeton, *The Crosswicks Horror.*" Now Oates intends to "completely rewrite" the latter book and also to publish a fifth and final volume she has written for the sequence, *My Heart Laid Bare,* which will "progress the 'Gothic' sequence up to the year of FDR's election, at which point I think I'll stop."[2] Her intent is "to create a highly complex structure in which individual novels (themselves complex in design, made up of 'books') functioned as chapters or units in an immense design: America as viewed through the prismatic lens of its most popular genres" (Preface to *MW,* 372–73).

Oates has before reimagined the works of famous progenitors: for example, the volume of short stories *Marriages and Infidelities* (1972) contains a number of such works. She has even written a book, *The Poisoned Kiss* (1975) by the imaginary author Fernandes, which she claims to have translated from the Portuguese. And, Oates's work has always been richly allusive, acknowledging openly its debt to the literary and intellectual traditions. Moreover, she has before written novels in series: *A Garden of Earthly Delights, Expensive People,* and *them* form a trilogy focusing on social groups in American society. Later novels—*Wonderland, Do With Me What You Will, The Assassins, Son of the Morning*—might be viewed as a kind of series on professionals in major institutions of American society: medicine, law, politics, religion.

But what is different about this undertaking is its immense scope and its playful, complex postmodernist technique. Whereas Oates's novels usually give allegiance to mimesis—to a credible rendering of social and psychological reality—these novels are gothicized fabulations that call attention to their own fictionality, inventiveness, and artifice. In their shifting of onto-logical levels, in their playful subtexts, in their idiosyncratic narrators and anachronistic style, in their intermingling of the plausible and the implausi-ble, surface and depth, the historical and the imagined, these works are technically postmodernist, if by postmodernist we mean that they are re-ceived by the reader as self-reflexive fictional constructions rather than as mimetic representations. Oates associates postmodernism with irony: she says of herself, "As a novelist of the 1980s, my vision is postmodernist and therefore predisposed to irony" ("Pleasure," 197). In her view "postmodern writing often gains a secondary meaning by its juxtaposition to other works of literature or art."[3] Such a secondary meaning is certainly gained through Oates's often tongue-in-cheek reimaginings of the popular nineteenth-century genres.

But I do not believe that any of Oates's works, including these novels, are more than technically postmodernist: indeed, she says herself that the novels "might be described as post-modernist in conception but thoroughly serious in execution" (Preface to *MW,* 372). Oates still has stories to tell and "com-plex propositions about the nature of personality" to put forward. Tech-nique is not an end in itself. However playfully imagined, these stories do not finally unravel into meaningless, self-reflexive simulacra as do some other postmodernist works. Oates does not reject all metanarratives—all-encompassing stories about all the stories we tell.[4] She remains committed to humanism and its metanarratives; that her view of the nature of personal-ity, for example, is shaped in part by one such metanarrative, Jung's, is evi-dent in these novels and others. These works are also about the need for psychic balance between the forces of the conscious and the unconscious, about the need for a relaxation of the polarization of the sexes. In short, al-though filtered through the prismatic lens of anachronistic genres, these novels, like all Oates's works, are serious studies of American character and American society. She says, "Primarily, each novel tells a story I consider uniquely American and of our time. The characters of the quartet are both our ancestors and ourselves" (Preface to *MW,* 372).

Oates claims that the "formal discipline of *genre* . . . forces us inevitably into a radical revisioning of the world of the craft of fiction." She says she found "irresistible" the attempt "to organize the voluminous material in patterns alien to my customary way of thinking and writing; to 'see' the world in terms of heredity and family destiny and the vicissitudes of Time (for all four of the novels are secretly fables of the American family); to ex-plore the historically authentic crimes against women, children, and the poor, in the guise of entertainment; to create, and to identify with, heroes and heroines whose existence could be problematic in the clinical, unkind, and, one might almost say, fluorescent-lit atmosphere of present-day fiction" (Preface to *MW*, 372–73). To reenvision American culture and history through its popular genres is to see more clearly its stridently patriarchal foundations and its pervasive misogyny. Such visions provoke Oates's ever more caustic feminist subtexts.

Bellefleur

The most impressive of these reworkings of nineteenth-century genres is the first, *Bellefleur,* which is among other things a brilliant reimagining of the family saga, using a technique that Oates has called experimental Gothic. She explains in the author's note to the volume, "This is a work of the imagination and must obey, with both humility and audacity, imagination's laws . . . the implausible is granted an authority and honored with a complexity usually reserved for realistic fiction . . . *Bellefleur* is a region, a state of the soul, and it does exist; and there, sacrosanct, its laws are utterly logical."[5] Indeed, in this novel Oates establishes herself as a magical realist to rival Gabriel Garcia Márquez. Alongside the dominant realistic mode are some wonderfully comic, absurdist, and supernatural touches effected through what Oates has called "the systematic transposition of realistic psychological and emotional experiences into 'Gothic' elements" (Preface to *B*, 370). Ghosts walk; spirits haunt; trolls bowl in the woods (one, Nightshade, becomes domesticated and gradually turns human); a vampire lives; a room is "contaminated"; the family patriarch insists that a drum be made from his skin after his death, and so it is; characters change dramatically in personality or physique, inexplicably getting taller or shorter, and one, Leah, is assured by her special mirror that she remains "the fairest of them all"; others drown, only to reappear years later; time "twists and coils and is, now, obliterated, and then again powerfully present" (author's note), causing differential aging: for example, Germaine grows from birth to age 4 while her father Gideon ages 20 to 30 years. The author explains the psychological realism implicit in this playfully imaginative Gothic technique:

We all experience mirrors that distort, we all age at different speeds, we have known people who want to suck our life's blood from us, like vampires; we feel haunted by the dead—if not precisely by the dead then by thoughts of them. We are forced at certain alarming periods of our lives not only to discover that other people are mysterious—and will remain mysterious—but that we ourselves, our motives, our passions, even our logic, are profoundly mysterious. . . . We are superstitious when events—usually coincidences—argue that "superstition" may be a way of grasping an essentially chaotic world. (Preface to *B*, 370–71)

The novel is, as Eileen Teper Bender astutely notes, "a transparency, a fabrication"⁶ displaying no allegiance to any single genre or to chronological time, fact, history, legend, or fable, but mixing them all together in a work of consummate imagination. The richly textured novel is also an encyclopedic conglomerate of interlocking tales—mountain legends, fairy tales, invented history—comprising a mythologic history of several generations of the powerful Bellefleur family and, through them, of America itself.

Fundamentally, the novel is what Oates has called a "complex parable of American aspirations and tragic shortcomings." It is reminiscent of Faulkner's *Absalom, Absalom!* in its legendized retelling of family tales, its historical scope, its rhetorical flourish, and its circuitous treatment of time (the epigraph to the volume is from Heraclitus: "Time is a child playing a game of draughts; the kingship is in the hands of a child"). Oates finds the perfect form for her "poetic vision" of the "American dream in both its daylight and nightmare aspects," in both conscious and unconscious dimensions, in both history and myth, in both dream and reality (Sjoberg, 116).

At the heart of the American dream is the quest for both material betterment and spiritual fulfillment—two goals that are not always complementary. The Bellefleurs epitomize and dramatize the dualities at the heart of the American dream and the American character.

What we gradually learn through the retelling of the Bellefleur stories is that like the great dynastic families of American history and legend, they wrenched out of the pristine wilderness, by ruthless, willful acquisition, a fortune and a foothold: the infamous Bellefleur "castle" sits astride their estate in what is now upper New York State. The patriarch, Jean-Pierre, early recognizes the nature of life in the new world: "*There is only one principle here as elsewhere, but here it is naked & cannot be deceived: the lust for acquisition: furs & timber: timber & furs: game: to snatch from this domain all it might yield greedy as men who have gone for days without eating suddenly ushered into a banquet hall & left to their own devices. One stuffs oneself, it is a frenzy, the lust to lay hands on everything, to beat out others, for the others are enemies*" (*B*, 534). This lust to acquire material possessions expresses itself across the generations of the Bellefleur family and sows the seeds of its own destruction—the desecration of the land, the avenging resentment of the exploited and dispossessed, the despairing emptiness and elusiveness of the quest.

Jean-Pierre establishes a dynasty, six generations of which are described in the novel, which spans the War of Independence to the present (a genealogy prefacing the volume helps to keep the scores of Bellefleurs straight). But the family is almost wiped out by the unacknowledged distaff side: the descendants of Brown Lucy, an early mistress. In 1825 her animalistic offspring rise up in murderous fury to eliminate Jean-Pierre, his current mistress, his son Louis, and three of his grandchildren.

The family is sustained through the eventual marriage of Louis's widow, Germaine, to Jedediah, the second of Jean-Pierre's sons. While his father and brothers had been amassing a fortune and conquering the wilderness, Jedediah had been on a 20-year quest for God, living like a hermit on Mount Blanc. The final scene of the novel circles back to this early time: Jedediah is called back by an "angel," a messenger from his brother Harlan, to sustain the family line and avenge the murders.

In his 20-year quest Jedediah expresses the other side of the American dream and the Bellefleur character, which appears in various manifestations across the succeeding generations—the quest for spiritual transcendence. Rather than aggrandizement of the family, the name, or the self, he seeks God. But this quest too is shown to be arrogant: Why should God show his face to Jedediah? In a truly deflating revelation, Jedediah experiences a ferocious "diarrheic spasm": "Where *Jedediah* had been now only streams and coils of scalding excrement remained." He realizes that "his entire lifetime, not simply these years on the mountain, had been nothing more than an organism's process, an outgoing ceaseless remorseless insatiable process—the gluttonous engorging of food, the digesting of food, the voiding of food." Moreover, the excrement is seething with white slugs: "The excrement *was* them, as it was himself." The relentless cycle of physical life is, Jedediah realizes, God's face: "So God showed His face to His servant Jedediah, and forever afterward kept His distance" (B, 440–41). This devastating epiphany recalls those experienced by characters in other Oates novels, such as Nathanael Vickery's vision of God as "a great hole, a great mouth" (SM, 362). Devouring jaws become a repeated motif, symbolizing the primordial bestiality at the heart of existence.

Yet Jedediah still wishes to maintain his hermitage, to escape the complications of human life: "I wanted only happiness—solitude—my own soul uncontaminated" (B, 558). But he is called back from this self-absorbed quest to join the human community, to unite with his widowed sister-in-law Germaine, whom he has always loved. His return is one of the many proofs that the forces of love are resilient.

Subsequent Bellefleur dreamers will also be tempted by the pull of an uncontaminated soul, away from the brutal competitiveness of life feeding on life, of dog eating dog, of jaws devouring jaws, of revenge spawning revenge. Several members of the family escape into the realm of the unconscious, most often by going into water. Raphael is mesmerized by Mink Pond and escapes the pursuing canine boy, Doan, by submerging himself in it. Lamentations of Jeremiah, disgusted over the greed of his family and the cannibalism of his silver foxes ("jaws devouring jaws"), walks into the flooded river as his mother Violet had years before: "Yet still he *wanted* to plunge into the storm, he *yearned* to submit himself to it, as if only so violent a baptism, far from the rude claims of *Bellefleur* and *blood,* could exorcise his memory of the foxes and their hideous blood jaws. *I am not one of you, as you see, the drowning man pleaded*" (B, 511). But he doesn't drown. Years later, as a nameless old man, he walks out of the river during another flood and, without assuming his old name and identity, remarries his former wife, Elvira, who is 100 years old. Vernon also tries to escape being a Bellefleur by seeming to drown in the river: "I am not a *Bellefleur,* I am only myself, Vernon, my essence is Vernon and not Bellefleur, I belong to God. I *am* God, God dwells in me . . . the poet . . . must take the chance of drowning in God" (B, 155). But apparently, he does not die either; his poetry, we learn later, continues to be produced. The cycle of life is eternal, and those who identify with it, Oates seems to imply, will share in its eternality.

Sometimes the pull of the dark other is sinister and malevolent. The Noir Vulture snatches Garnet's child. Lake Noir is full of the whisperings and proddings of nighttime spirits, which, for example, drive the murderers of Jean-Pierre and his clan into a frenzy: "the men had lost control of themselves, they hadn't been able to stop until everyone was dead. Until all the Bellefleurs lay lifeless, smashed and bleeding" (B, 456).

Great-uncle Hiram is haunted by a capricious night self that differs starkly from his fastidious day self and leads him into nocturnal ventures, including one in which he is drawn to Lake Noir in the winter and observes beneath the ice "a figure who [is] upside down, and whose feet [are] evidently pressed against his" (B, 526). Leah, in uncharacteristic despondency, feels herself to be floating "bodiless, at the bottom of a great dark pool of water. She was the drowned Vernon, she was Violet, she was Jeremiah who had been swept away in a flood. What remained of *Leah* cared to protest nothing" (B, 407).

The attractions and the dangers of the other take many playful and imaginative shapes. Characters pass over into other realms, becoming embodiments of their strongest desires or most dominant traits. Yolande, who runs away from home as a young girl, reappears later as a celluloid image, a movie star on the screen; she seems to have no other existence. Samuel, infatuated by the "Room of Contamination," which holds alien spirits —especially that of the dark, sensuous other, the Negro—goes over irretrievably to the other side. Tamas disappears into the clavichord he lovingly makes for Violet. Hepatica's husband, a brutish man, turns into a bear; Johnny Doan, a canine boy, becomes a dog; Veronica's lover, excessively attentive, is a vampire. Through such Gothic elements, Oates imaginatively and symbolically dramatizes the dialectics of the self and other, man and nature, good and evil, consciousness and unconsciousness, and the contradictory strains in the American dream.

Indeed, the main plot line dramatizes these dualities. The dominant characters of the novel, Gideon and Leah, are cousins locked in a marriage rent by the self-destructiveness of a family absorbed by itself, divided against itself, and set in willful opposition to others and to nature. Leah, a beautiful earth mother, is totally corrupted by the acquisitive scheming; she feels it is her task to restore the former glory of the Bellefleurs, and she uses the extrasensory powers of her daughter Germaine to attempt to further these ends. Gideon is a driven and unhappy man who uses and abuses women and who pursues a self-destructive course that ends in his deliberately crashing an airplane into the Bellefleur Manor (the conflagration of which parallels the inevitable fate of the dynastic mansions in Faulkner's mythic world). Germaine's powers, like Mink Pond, appear to be emblematic of a natural and instinctual link to nature—a gift that is lost as the Bellefleurs abuse life. Gradually, Germaine becomes a normal child and Mink Pond decays and disappears.

But the family is not wiped out. As Oates explains, "The elder members of the powerful Bellefleur family are destroyed but, one by one their children—who may represent a younger or at any rate more selfless and idealistic America—escape their influence and achieve their independence apart from the family's authority" (Sjoberg, 116). The novel is, Oates claims, "a critique of America; but it is in the service of a vision of America that stresses, for all its pessimism, the ultimate freedom of the individual" (*Preface to B,* 371). As Bromwell Bellefleur puts it, the survivors are "condemned to sanity. His rejection of the remorseless claims of blood [is] but one aspect of his sanity" (*B,* 545). Oates calls the novel both comic and tragic. While many characters are destroyed, it is "a comedy in the higher sense that the instinct for survival and self-determination is celebrated" (Sjoberg, 116). In true comedic fashion, the novel ends with marriages: that of Garth and Goldie, who "wanted to live somewhere where no one knew the name *Bellefleur,*" on a farm in Nebraska; that of Garnet and Lord

Dunraven; and Christabel's marriage to her beloved, Demuth Godge, rather than to her mother's choice, Edgar, and to his fortune of adjacent land, as Leah had grandly schemed. And, as mentioned earlier, the last episode of the novel circles back in time to note Jedediah's return from Mount Blanc to marry Germaine and so to perpetuate the family line.

This reconstructed narrative, however, does a disservice to the nonnarrative design of the book and to its richly experimental and imaginative technique, its melodious and grandiloquent language, its dense and complicated plots, its host of eccentric characters, its sheer exuberance and playfulness. I agree with John Gardner's assessment of this novel: "it is simply brilliant . . . a magnificent piece of daring, a tour de force of imagination and intellect."[7] *Bellefleur* should be recognized for what it undoubtedly is: one of our great American novels.

A Bloodsmoor Romance

The second novel in the series, *A Bloodsmoor Romance,* is a parody both of the genre of the romance novel and of the ideas and social attitudes toward women that the genre reflected. Its parodic subtext is feminist as well as ribald. Like *Bellefleur,* this novel is a fabrication calling attention to its artifice; conflating ontological levels; intermingling fictional, literary, and historical and fantastical characters and events; reveling in its postmodernist intertextuality. The novel purports to be a turn-of-the-century romance, narrated in a breathless and mannerly style by a maiden of advanced years—one of Hawthorne's "damn horde of scribbling women," no doubt. She often intersperses her salubrious tale with heartfelt exclamations of sentiment, honey-coated platitudes, and moral maxims. Indeed, the novel is as much about her response to the stories she narrates as it is about the stories themselves. While the old-fashioned authoress attempts to tell her tale, her irreverent twentieth-century counterpart, Joyce Carol Oates, breaks illusion of realism, burlesques the norms, and develops a witty feminist subtext.

Focusing on the lives of several members of the Kiddemaster and Zinn family, the novel is densely situated within the changing culture of the last 20 years of nineteenth-century American history. It intersperses the story of John Quincy Zinn, the embodiment of au courant ideas at the turn of the century, with that of the women of his family, who are literally and figuratively confined within the domestic sphere and within the restrictive and prescriptive roles dictated by the patriarchy.

John Quincy Zinn, of inauspicious beginnings—he is orphaned when his Yankee-peddler father is brutally tarred and feathered—becomes a

moderately famous inventor. At age 18 he is thrilled by Emerson's trans-
cendentalism and convinced that his unique destiny is linked to the ever-
expansive American Destiny. "*America,* he state[s], and *Invention* are
near-synonymous!"[8] He revels in American inventions: the telegraph, the
steam engine, the cotton gin, the reaper. He confidently anticipates the invention of the submarine, the horseless carriage, the airplane. America,
Zinn proudly announces to the schoolchildren he teaches, is "a new Garden of Eden" (*BR,* 208). He gains some attention in educational circles in
Philadelphia when he writes a report about his country school-teaching,
Out of the Mouths of Babes: A Teacher's Day-Book, which emphasizes spon-
taneity and creativity as a mode of instruction: "All effort in a child is creative . . . and all creativity is good" (*BR,* 205). Concomitant with his
insatiable concern with invention, however, is sometimes a careless disre-
gard for life. While working on his time machine, his young student
Nahum Hareton (a character borrowed from *Wuthering Heights*) crawls
inside it and spins out of existence "quite as if he had never been born; for,
indeed, under these circumstances, he never *had* been born" (*BR,* 219).

Zinn also has no compunctions about experimenting on his daughter
Samantha; he removes her birthmark (recalling Hawthorne's story "The
Birthmark"). She does not die as a result, but she deeply resents his presumption. Gradually, Zinn is corrupted by a monomanical compulsion for
inventing: more and more, he focuses on instruments of destruction. Although initially repelled when approached by the United States government
about making a "humane" instrument of execution, he does finally devise
the electric chair. Near the end of his life his idea of a perpetual-motion machine is corrupted into an idea for "*an endless series of detonations*"—an
atomic bomb, which he madly rationalizes (like others to follow) will keep
peace in the world.

Zinn's mad science, then, sounds a discordant and ominous note. It is
one of the many ways in which the rapidly changing world of late-Victorian
America spills beyond the platitudes and conventions of the domestic romance. While the narrator attempts to tie up neatly all the pieces of her
story, she seems aware of how tenuous is her closure and how depleted the
romance for the new world dawning at the turn of the century. At the end of
the novel she says, "Beyond this I cannot—indeed, I do not wish—to ven-
ture, for the Twentieth Century is not my concern" (*BR,* 615).

Indeed, the narrator at several points readily acknowledges that the story
she tells exceeds her capacity to do so; she often flutters prissily before embarrassing disclosures. She attributes this to her inferiority as a woman,
which renders her "so generally unfit for the creation of great works, like

those of Mr. Dickens and Mr. Balzac, and in our own clime Mr. Melville"
(*BR,* 522). Through both the narrator and Edwina Kiddemaster, an
authoress in the novel, Oates dramatizes the barriers women faced in attempting to write a "literature of their own."[9] Women, in fact, are willing
instruments of the patriarchy, schooling other women in self-deprecation
and self-imposed limitations. Edwina Kiddemaster spends her life writing
etiquette and advice books for young women, urging them to inhibit both
their minds and their bodies in order to please men: "gentlemen are naturally discomforted by an *excess of ratiocination,* in the weaker sex," she
claims. So too are women told that "the *physical* by its very nature is *gross,*
and that the flesh of the female sex, whilst required for habitation on this
earth, is yet angelic in aspiration, and partakes not at all of the lusty carnal
appetites of the male" (*BR,* 443).

Oates reduces to the absurd this equation of the feminine with a denial of
appetite. Grandmother Sarah Kiddemaster, a model of feminine anorexia,
is found when she dies to be nearly hollow, with miniaturized or absent internal organs. Moreover, when alive, she had occupied her time with appropriate female busywork: prior to her death she had been working on an
antimascassar three-quarters of a mile long!

The novel centers on the romances of five Zinn sisters, a group of daughters paralleled loosely, in Oates's playful allusion, with the range of female
types in Alcott's *Little Women*. These types are carried to burlesque ex-
tremes, exposing the hand of the irreverent twentieth-century novelist, who
undercuts the romance and demonstrates a tenacious degree of "feminist
resistance"—escapist strategies both deliberately and fortuitously employed
by the Zinn sisters.

The most submissive and compliant of the daughters, Octavia, marries
with the proper attitude, inspiring the narrator's gushing sentiment: "Loving, unquestioning obedience! Dependence! Cheerful resignation! What can
be sweeter? To submit oneself wholly and contentedly into the hands of another; to surrender all appetite for the grossness of Self: to cease taking
thought about oneself at all, and rest in safe harbor" (*BR,* 369). With
steadfast and uncritical wifely duty, Octavia puts up with the ever more bi-
zarre, perverse, and abusive lovemaking routines of her sanctimonious and
kinky husband, the Reverend Rumford, who has her dress in hood, corset,
petticoat, and numerous pretty accoutrements. But the Reverend does himself in one day when he commands Octavia to pull ever tighter a noose
around his neck: he chokes to death in the "unitary act." Thus, one feels that
Oates is ironically meting out justice. Later she rewards virtue as well, mat-
ing Octavia with a sexually attractive young man.

Octavia's eldest sister, Constance Phillipe, who is married off to Baron von Mainz, absconds on the night of her wedding—a wise move, one thinks, considering the fate of Baron von Mainz's two previous wives, both of whom had died mysteriously and been found, like Grandmother Kiddemaster, to be hollow women with withered internal organs; both had been carrying stone fetuses as well. Constance Phillipe leaves a dressmaker's dummy in her place in the marital bed, an exchange her husband doesn't notice until after the consummation of their marriage (the headless, limbless dummy is only one of many such surrogates for women in this novel). Finding the ultimate path of rebellion against woman's fate, Constance Phillipe is Alcott's tomboy with a vengeance: she dons male attire, assumes a male's life-style, and then actually turns into a man—or so the narrator tells us, although she claims to be "*ignorant of all detail, and wish[ing] to remain so*" (*BR,* 582).

Brainy Samantha—like Rappacinni's daughter and like Louisa May Alcott to her father, Bronson Alcott—serves as a guinea pig for her mad-scientist father, who removes her birthmark when she is a baby. But poetic justice is later served when she falls in love and runs off with another of his victims, Nahum Hareton, who has reappeared after having been reeled out of existence for a while in Zinn's time machine. Later, tongue-in-cheek, Oates shows Samantha's inventiveness manifested in life-affirming, if domestic, products: a baby-mobile, a bicycle-umbrella, and disposable diapers.

Malvina, aspiring actress and femme fatale, has "the mark of the beast"—a shameful incapacity to suppress her sexuality and physicality. She tries in lovemaking to lie "immobile, as if paralyzed, or a veritable corpse, the better to overcome unspeakable inclinations," but inevitably the "demonic caprices of body" take over, often reversing sexual roles and overwhelming her lovers, including the lusty Mark Twain, who runs away in horror from "that bed of bestial extremities" (*BR,* 465). Malvina turns to celibacy for relief and later marries the devoted Mr. Kennicott on the condition that they will live as brother and sister.

Another kind of mark of the beast is on Deirdre, the adoptive daughter, who has psychic powers and connections to the spirit world. She is inexplicably whisked off early in the novel in a hot-air balloon, only to appear later as the medium Deirdre of the Shadows, an acquaintance of Madame Blavatsky. She is the artist figure who experiences the permeable boundaries between one being and another, who can descend into the unconscious. Alien in both the Zinn family and in the male-dominated larger world, she is the dark, dangerous other. A study of her by the male Society for Psychical Research ends disastrously, with two scientists being mutilated to death by spirits. Deirdre is overtaken and for a time driven mad by the spirits who possess her. Later, true to well-worn romantic convention, she is shown to be the long-lost child—the daughter of Edwina Kiddemaster and heiress to her estate. She shares her new wealth with her sisters, yet it is not clear that she can overcome a lifetime of rejection and be successfully integrated into a life of ordinary womanhood, ordinary domesticity. The split that she feels is dramatized in her inability to choose between two suitors, the Anglo-Saxon Dr. Stoughton and the Indian Hassan Agha.

The novel ends with a kind of unsettling standoff between the world of romance convention and the world of the madman's science, between the conscious and unconscious parts of Deirdre's nature, between the patriarchy's dictates and feminist resistance. While her sisters are paired off in happy twosomes—and while even Prudence, Zinn's wife, has belatedly found her "love," a passionate commitment to the women's suffrage movement—Deirdre is left tending the sick Zinn in the final scene of the novel. But in an action shrouded in ambiguity, in which she says that "*a spirit hand of near-miniature proportions, possessing prehensile fingers, and o'erlong nails not unlike claws, grasped hold of her wrist, and forced the paper down inside the glass, and into the flame!*" she destroys the formula for atomic fusion, which she had recovered from the laboratory for Zinn. She thinks excitedly, "'And, should it *not* be duplicated . . . will I not then have *saved the world?* Spared us, from the madman's dream?'—tho' in the next breath she chided herself, and bit her lip, for having uttered so blasphemous a statement" (*BR*, 614). Women, and the dark powers to which they are linked, seem to have temporarily, if self-deprecatingly, triumphed.

A Bloodsmoor Romance is, for the most part, a witty reimagining of the domestic romance, with a playful feminist subtext. But the mad undercurrents are there as well, threatening to overturn conventional order. Science can be turned to humanity's betterment or destruction. Similarly, the unconscious, emblematized by Deirdre's dark powers, is a potent mystery yet to be understood.

Mysteries of Winterthurn

Oates's next novel in this series, *Mysteries of Winterthurn*, is much more caustically feminist, although the genre of the novel, like most aspects of it, is duplicitous. The novel is at one level a set of triple-decker detective mysteries with a male questor, Xavier Kilgarvan, who solves mysteries by using American pragmatism and the best of investigative crime-detection methods. Yet Xavier repeatedly comes up against the dark underside of the stridently patriarchal world, and its darkness is inevitably connected with women and with crimes against women. This aspect of the male-dominated society is alluded to in Oates's explanation of the genesis of her mysteries:

Each of the mysteries is based upon composite cases. The first is derived primarily from a small, disturbing item I saw in the paper—several mummified infants were found in the attic of an elderly maiden lady, after her death. She'd lived with an older brother for most of her life. The second mystery is derived from a number of serial murderers whose victims were young girls. The Klan-like organization is, in fact, based upon the Ku Klux Klan, which came into being, historically, in a way paralleling the novel's narrative, as the consequence of the lynching of the Jewish foreman [Leo Frank] of a factory in, I believe Atlanta. . . . The third mystery is based upon a notorious New Brunswick, N.J. case of the 1920's, sensationally known as the "case of the minister and the choir singer." That's to say, an amalgam of this case, and Lizzie Borden, and very likely one or two others."[10]

The three tales in *Mysteries of Winterthurn* were supposedly collected by a self-proclaimed "amateur 'collector' of Murder." The tales are set more than a century prior to the narration, in the closing decades of the nineteenth century. All feature Xavier Kilgarvan, detective sui generis, who ages and changes through the harrowing experiences of trying to solve the Winterthurn mysteries. He starts off as an adolescent eager to match the feats of his detective heroes: Sherlock Holmes, C. Auguste Dupin, George B. Jashber, and Pudd'nhead Wilson, as well as ambiguous heroes of pulp novelettes. While he has a brilliant career outside of Winterthurn City, he is done in, finally, by the intractable mysteries within the locale of his birth— indeed, within his own family and his own being. By the end of the novel, he has at the age of 40 sworn off mystery and Winterthurn for life and matrimony in exile.

The novel is a fictional amplification of a statement Oates made in her essay "At Least I Have Made a Woman of Her": "A man's quarrel with Women is a quarrel with himself—with those 'despised' and muted elements in his personality which he cannot freely acknowledge because they challenge his sense of masculine supremacy and control."[11] Oates comments: "I found the history of criminology and forensic science an intriguing parallel with the history of civilization. Brilliant criminals are always one step ahead of the law—at least until they're caught" (letter, 16 July 1990). Over the course of the three stories Xavier unwittingly becomes a malevolent participant in the avenging world of women. What is gradually revealed is that "sex wars, not the fun kind,"[12] are taking a bloody toll.

In the first of the three interrelated stories and mysteries, "The Virgin in the Rose-Bower; or, the Tragedy of Glen Mawr Manor," the question is, Who is committing the murders in the Honeymoon Room? The story is full of mysteries and mystification, and it is uncertain which genre we are in. Detective fiction is a genre of control, of answers and solutions; it celebrates the triumph of ratiocination over mystery. In this novel the detective genre is, however, mixed with Gothic romance. The permeable boundaries between the genres are only one example of shifting boundaries; there are also those between natural and supernatural, good and evil, past and present, animate and inanimate, living and dead, real and fanciful, one person and another, this story and its literary precursors. Here, possession by evil ghosts of previous generations, attacks by dead infants who have been turned into angel-demons, and the like must be considered along with more realistic interpretations.

The story catalogues a series of horrific events connected to the Kilgarvans of Glen Mawr Manor, including savage murders and attacks in the Honeymoon Room. Reminiscent of the Room of Contamination in *Bellefleur,* the lavishly appointed Honeymoon Room has a trompe l'oeil painting from which angel-devils seem to emerge to attack guests in the room. Indeed, in the first incident of the book, the back of a child's head is grossly eaten away.

The story induces vertigo for both Xavier and the reader because of the difficulty of getting to a satisfactory "solution" of the mystery and mystification. The supernatural explanations, although mocked, are the ones that make the most sense: the boundaries between living and dead, animate and inanimate are permeable. In the manner of Hawthorne, there is extreme obfuscation and mystification—a kind of teasing of multiple interpretations, multiple possibilities. Also, the very epistemological grounds of the story are questioned. Simon Esdras, the brother of Erasmus, achieves some notoriety as author of a philosophical *Treatise on the Probable "Existence" of the World,* which is published in a series of editions, each time with a different element in the title bracketed, calling into question ontological levels of reality.

It is never clear whether time periods are distinct from each other. It seems to be relevant, for example, that generations ago Hester Vaugh had been condemned as a murderess for abandoning her illegitimate child, although she was held by feminists to be a victim. She vows revenge, and one feels that her avenging spirit haunts the used and abused women of the novel. Rococo in mystery and mystification, "The Virgin in the Rose-

Bower" is full of miscellaneous infant deaths, mutilated corpses, poisoned husbands, and mad women.

When Xavier finally puts all the pieces of the story together, he must conclude that Judge Erasmus Kilgarvan perpetuated in his household gross use and abuse of his wives and daughters. The victims blame themselves, never him, for their "evil." Apparently tortured and beaten, full of self-contempt, both his wives go mad before their deaths; the second wife commits suicide. Judge Kilgarvan apparently sexually violated his eldest daughter, Georgina, and probably also abused his two younger daughters, Perdita and Therese, who remain "possessed" by him. Georgina apparently birthed five infants, strangled them with wire, and put them in drawers in the attic above the Honeymoon Room. The spirits of these infants apparently animate the angels in the trompe l'oeil painting in the Honeymoon Room, which turning into devilish creatures who attack and kill guests in the room or drive them mad.

These angel-demons act out an important theme of the novel: thwarted love turns to demonic evil. "Angels *may* turn demon, with the passage of time,—if starved of love that is their sustenance."[13] Georgina must kill her children in order to preserve the appearance of domestic normality in the patriarchal household, just as she must kill in herself any pretense to normal selfhood. She rejects a suitor and stops publishing poems at her father's command, although her poetry, akin to that of Emily Dickinson, achieves posthumous success. Her pseudonym is Iphigenia, an appropriate name-sake, since her life is sacrificed to patriarchal dictates. Finally she too commits suicide.

Xavier is so horrified by the vertiginous nature of events, so appalled by what he learns about Judge Kilgarvan, and so confused by his love for Perdita that he destroys his detective notes. The nightmarish underside of domesticity is not exposed.

The second story, "Devil's Half-Acre; or, The Mystery of the 'Cruel Suitor,'" takes place 12 years later. While the first story centered on the strange happenings in the Honeymoon Room, this story's haunted and cursed place is a half acre where a defrocked preacher of a minor heretic sect, Elias Fenwick (nicknamed "the Bishop"), was said to have held witches' masses in 1759. The story is reminiscent of Hawthorne's "Young Goodman Brown" in that the good citizens of Winterthurn display their secret evil propensities. Now the land where Fenwick is buried is the site of the deaths of a number of young girls, and the mystery Xavier seeks to solve is the identity of the "Cruel Suitor."

Infused with antifeminism and well as anti-Semitism, public opinion has it that the victims were women of doubtful reputation and promiscuous sexual behavior and that the cruel suitor is a Jew, Isaac Rosenwald, who is finally lynched. Xavier quickly rejects these unlikely suppositions and conclusions and realizes that the murderer is dandy Valentine Westergaard. The question is, How to prove it?

But Xavier's confidence in the powers of ratiocination and logical investigation is again upset by the vertiginous nature of reality and the shifting ontological levels of the story. In an important episode, he is tricked by the planting of a seeming clue—a glove—in the Bishop's half acre, and sinks into quicksand. Part of the mystery is that we never learn precisely how he gets out. We do know that the experience is profoundly unsettling, that Xavier feels he has lost his hold on immediate reality and is adrift in the *"primordial, everlasting, boundaryless* Universe." He loses his sense of differentiated individuality and selfhood. He is confronted with the greatest of mysteries, for which there is no ready answer: What is the nature of the Universe? Confusing the ontological levels of the story, Xavier seems to be aware of himself as a character in a story: *"incongruous, unseemly, unnatural*—that I should die now, in the midst of the story" (*MW,* 259, 258).

Most upsetting to Xavier is the ultimate deflation of his idealistic belief that detective work is an intelligent, pragmatic, and systematic unification with the forces of God. He sees the detective's search for truth as a paradigm for all academic disciplines, that "life itself could be imagined as a pursuit, a hunt, an impassioned quest requiring diligence and bravery and resignation." Peregrine calls Xavier a Platonist who wants to rid the world of criminality, while he himself deals with a morally checkered world, not a lost Eden from which we are expelled (*MW,* 304).

Xavier's triumph seems assured when he gathers irrefutable evidence that Valentine Westergaard is the murderer, but things go askew at the trial. Shockingly, Xavier's own brother Colin is implicated as an accomplice, and Westergaard testifies that he was the unwilling perpetrator of the crimes, possessed by a malevolent personage, an enemy to both God and man, long dead but known—the evil "Bishop" Fenwick, who invaded his being and demanded five "brides." The story seems to give credence to the view, put forward by Herbert Spencer, that there may lurk within each individual "an *older, incoherent, bestial,* and altogether *amoral* 'ancestor,' scarcely known or intuited by the waking mind, but parasitic upon it, and highly dangerous: indeed capable of monstrous eructation of violence" (*MW,* 194).

Moreover, many people blame the victims, believing these factory girls got what they deserved. These young women "unmanned" Westergaard, "*so determined to provoke manly rage* in their thrashing and sobbing and bloody discharges!" (*MW*, 324). The misogyny of society knows no bounds; it is pervasively infused in all social institutions: family, law, medicine, recreation. Dr. Colney Hatch (named slyly after a famous lunatic asylum in England), Winterthurn's eminent physician, has been assembling for twenty years evidence pertaining to the diverse weaknesses of women and the general inferiority of the sex—findings *"precisely analogous"* to those later published by Freud (*MW*, 231). Indeed, gynecology is a science of torture and denigration.

Westergaard is acquitted and leaves town with a veiled lady (who, we are told incidentally in the last story of the volume, dies an unnatural death). Incredulous and demoralized, Xavier receives the ultimate insult—a note from Valentine, who is at his Northern Italian vacation spot enjoying the "exotic & somewhat agreeable *divertissements* of the Marital Bed," with this message: "The 'Bishop' having assuredly decamped from *my* being, pray, sweet Xavier, he does not next settle into *yours*" (*MW*, 349). Indeed, Xavier had earlier found evidence that Valentine thinks of him as his doppelgänger, his double (*MW*, 284). These linkages seem to portend Xavier's implication in the evil he studies. Therese tries to tell him that his error was in thinking that Valentine acted alone. All these clues suggest that perhaps evil cannot be located in a single source; perhaps it does not yield to ready solution.

The narrator of the mystery also seems demoralized by the turn of events. After "withdrawing, by degrees, from the piteous scene"—backing away, as it were, from Xavier and giving him a resigned "farewell"—the narrator ends the tale "with infinite relief" (*MW*, 346). There continues to be a very poor fit between the neat shape of detective fiction and the inchoate mystery that surrounds events.

Given the pervasive misogyny of society, it is little wonder that Perdita is convinced of her morally weak nature and her "sin-stained Soul." The sisters Perdita and Therese represent the perdition and faith, as their names suggest. Perdita displays the darker side of feminine nature, although to a modern she seems quite natural, if a little indiscreet, in her equivocal flirtation with Xavier. Perdita decides to marry a "spiritual bridegroom," Reverend Bunting, and to resist Xavier, whose occupation "leads [him] to an unwholesome contemplation of Evil, & an indifference to God" (*MW*, 335–36). Yet echoing *Wuthering Heights,* Perdita testifies to a passionate, primordial attachment to Xavier, akin to Catherine's for Heathcliff: "'I, abandon *you!* Why, it is as much a possibility,' she said vehemently, 'as the earth detaching itself from the sun, and veering off, of its own wild volition, into the depthless and lightless abyss of *Nothing!*'" (*MW*, 338).

This thwarting of love, like many other acts in the novel, appears to carry in its wake a demonic revenge, detailed in the final story of the volume, "The Bloodstained Bridal Gown; or, Xavier Kilgarvan's Last Case." The story centers on the murder of Perdita's husband, Reverend Bunting, who is found in a compromising position with another corpse, that of Mrs. Amanda Poindexter, a matron of the parish. Also murdered is Reverend Bunting's mother, and Perdita claims to have been forced into her bridal gown and brutally raped.

The editor's note prefacing the tale holds to an optimistic view that "the mystery or detective novel boldly upholds the principle, *in defiance of contemporary sentiment,* that infinite Mystery, beyond that of the finite, may yield to human ratiocination: that truth will 'out': that happiness is possible once Evil is banished: and that God, though it seems, withdrawn at the present time from both Nature and History, is yet a living presence in the world." The narrator asserts that the detective "is the very emblem of our souls, a sort of mortal savior, not only espying but isolating, and conquering Evil; in his triumph is our triumph." The story hardly bears out this triumphant assertion. As a result of the events of the story, Xavier gives up his "accursed" profession. The narrator rather patly asserts that the "appalling mystery is handily resolved: the murderer, unlike Valentine Westergaard, does not escape God's wrath: and peace and tranquility are restored to a distressed community. In addition *a happy ending is provided,*—one both plausible and deserved" (*MW,* 353–55).

This tidying up, however, is not convincing. With many loose ends and unexplained mysteries, the story unravels. Oates explains, "My 'mystery-detective' fiction is meant, though I hope not distractingly, to be a critique of the genre, from within. As a reader, I am always restless and disappointed in such books, as they near their conclusions; yet I'm always excited at the outset. (As during the first ten minutes or so of a movie, when everything seems possible—before the rigors of plot close in" (letter, 16 July 1990). Rather than serving as an emblem of man's triumph over circumstances ("I make my circumstance," Xavier's card, quoting Emerson, boldly claims), detective fiction is shown to be an inadequate genre of control and order; the narrator's pat assurances do not ring true.

Xavier believes initially that Mr. Poindexter has perpetrated the crimes, perhaps by using the iceman, Jabez Dovekie, as his agent. Xavier follows his man outside the city limits of Winterthurn to the Hotel Paradise, a pleasure spot that is a kind of free zone for men of "all social ranks,—a lawless, and, indeed, unlicensed place where vices of every imaginable sort . . . [are] freely indulged." Hotel Paradise is in fact a "hellish sort of 'Paradise' . . .

wherein pleasure has no limit," as Xavier thinks. Here is the misogynous underside of this society, where women are subjected to unspeakable horrors in "cork-lined subterranean chambers, wherein instruments of torture [are] available,—whips, and branding irons, and makeshift gallows, and 'operating tables'" (MW, 452, 456). Here is the dark underside of human consciousness, only fleetingly acknowledged by the conscious mind. Here women are schooled in guilt and depravity. Here Xavier discovers the sickly mulatto child of Ellery Poindexter. Poindexter, so enraged by Xavier's hunting down of him, dies of an apparent heart attack, "suffocating, as it were, upon his own fury" (MW, 463).

Xavier, shortly after the death of Ellery Poindexter, falls into "some sort of debilitating illness" and continues to be obsessed by the circumstances surrounding the murders. Finally, he declares to his friend Murre Pitt-Davies "that it had been he, and not Ellery Poindexter after all, who had committed the murders." He claims that he had "cunningly arranged to appear to arrive in Winterthurn" after the murderers "in order to consummate a secret design" (MW, 472).

At least one critic, Cara Chell, believes him. She argues that Perdita and Xavier had planned the murders and that Xavier had been the "Red-Haired Specter" who carried them out.[14] Clues about Xavier's implication do indeed abound. I think the point, though, is that Xavier more and more discovers that he, as well as others, does not "make his circumstance," that the mystery of human nature, including his own, is inscrutable. He is said to have alcohol-induced trances followed by total amnesia. He repeatedly refers to his "death" in the quicksand; his "soul" appears to be lost. Perhaps the implication is that his spirit, starved for love like that of the demon-angels in the first story, turns demonic. Apparently, the incident in the quicksand upsets his sense of "masculine control and supremacy": he seems to experience "an uncalibrated shifting of planes, an actual rent (as it were) in the fabric of Reality itself!" (MW, 257). He experiences, in effect, the death of his conscious self and is opened up to the unconscious and to participation in the realm of lost souls, a realm populated by used and abused women.

Moreover, Winterthurn seems to Xavier to be the place of his "damnation." His mother had pronounced a curse upon him: "that he wander the earth for the remainder of his life, unless some woman, as wicked as he, offer him love" (MW, 403). Perdita offers that love and assists in the murders of her husband, his mistress, and his mother, showing a dark, rebellious side that belies her appearance. Confirming this interpretation, Oates comments:

Perdita is the murderess of the last mystery. Like Lizzie Borden, who, as a lady, could not be imagined as having killed both her parents, Perdita is spared by the sexist attitudes of her era. For a while, Xavier successfully blocks this knowledge; then he succumbs to it, has a breakdown, but, in the end, recovers—and marries Perdita. So too I've felt that, in life, in much more subtle (and surely unarticulated) ways, we give in finally to that which we've imagined was antithetical to us, and unassimilatable (if that is a word!). (letter, 16 July 1990)

Certainly, Perdita has cause for her rebellion; she is subjected to the brutalization of her father, the perversities and unfaithfulness of her husband, the restrictions of her female role as dictated by male authorities. The crowning blow seems to be her thwarted desire to adopt a sickly child, whom her husband and doctor decide to let die. The ubiquitous infant deaths in this novel are horrible signs of the thwarting of love. Perdita's "good" side—which is capable of being a healthy, normal, passionate, and loving young woman—is overtaken by a willful, rebellious, vengeful self.

Echoing *Wuthering Heights,* Perdita is haunted by a specter trying to get in through her window: "I am wicked,—I have sinned,—even if I have not sinned, why, I *am* wicked . . . so he shall come for me: and naught but a thin pane of glass separates us" (*MW,* 363). The specter's presence, like that of the ghosts in James's *The Turn of the Screw,* is confirmed by the faithful servant, Nell: "It was poor Nell's fancy that she did see him, or it,—though for but a fleeting instant, upon that occasion. A most diabolical agent, in that his countenance seemed *angelic!*—and his features regular and cleanly chiseled, like those of a statue of olden times" (*MW,* 418). As in the fractured world of *Wuthering Heights,* the violation of the primordial passion of the lovers carries a toll of misery, violence, and destruction. When the lovers are united, like Catherine and Hareton at the end of *Wuthering Heights,* the violence abates and domesticity prevails.

Oates is, of course, writing with the license that a postmodernist's reimagining of a nineteenth-century genre allows, yet she puts us in an uncomfortable position. Do we champion the murderous liberation of Perdita and Xavier? The book recalls the problematic "violent liberation" of Jules Wendall in *them.* About Jules, Oates said, "He is both a hero and a murderer at once. I think that is ironic. I hope it is."[15] The same might be said of Xavier and Perdita. Xavier needs to lose his male conscious and rational control and plunge into Perdita's lost female world. With his help she turns her maternal heritage of madness, repression, and victimization into a violent and problematic liberation. As Georgina's children exact revenge for

their thwarted lives, so does Perdita. The sex wars of Winterthurn are every
bit as bloody as the class wars of Detroit.

As Sandra Gilbert and Susan Gubar have trenchantly demonstrated, the
"received and unexamined" bifurcated images of women in our cultural and
literary heritage—the angel and the monster, Jane Eyre and Bertha, Snow
White and the Wicked Queen—are two halves of the same female identity.[16] By embracing rather than denying the dark side of her being, by
using cunning and violence, by drawing in Xavier's assistance, Perdita is
saved from perdition and liberated into normal domesticity. Neither angel
nor demon, she embraces a complex selfhood.

Having said that, I must add that it is hard to overestimate how teasingly
playful this book is, with its shifting ontological levels, conflating of genres,
and interweaving of the plots of famous stories. Yet here as in the two earlier
parodies, Oates's intent is to use highly imaginative fabrications to comment seriously on aspects of American society and American character. *Mysteries of Winterthurn* is Oates's most virulent exposé of the misogynistic and
stereotypical views of women implicit in our literary and cultural heritage.

Both *A Bloodsmoor Romance* and *Mysteries of Winterthurn* show women
struggling with the limitations of authorship, creativity, and selfhood imposed on them by stereotypes that bifurcate female possibility into value-
laden opposites. To be good is to be submissive, selfless, and sexless. To be
bad is to be willful, passionate, and sexual. The bifurcation, unless escaped,
leads to repression, emptiness, and madness. When Oates switches back
into the realistic mode—as she does in her next three novels, *Solstice,
Marya: A Life,* and *You Must Remember This*—she situates the drama in the
warring dualities of female identity itself.

Chapter Four
Dualities of Female Identity

I have argued that Oates's short stories and novels are populated by a host of unliberated women—inarticulate, imperceptive victims of an inadequate model of female selfhood.[1] Yet the early Oates was not usually thought of as a feminist writer. She did not call attention to herself as a woman thinking and writing about women. Indeed, for years she found it annoying and insulting when the sexist label of "woman writer" was applied to her. She wrote, she insisted, within broad contexts and traditions unrestricted by gender.[2] She has always found sexist and insulting the question (often asked of her) "Why is your writing so violent?" Writing, she insists, is "a wholly neutral—or do I mean neuter?—genderless activity." She never assumed that Emily Dickinson's poetry, for example, was the product of a female consciousness, "for didn't it mean that, being a poet, having been granted the imprimatur of poet, Emily Dickinson had in fact transcended not only the 'female' but the 'human' categories?" ("Pleasure," 61).

Joyce Carol Oates is now much more realistic about how she will inevitably be perceived, about how deeply ingrained sexist labeling is in our culture. In both her fiction and her essays, she participates in feminist discourse by attempting to assess how women are made and unmade by male definitions of womanhood. Now she says unequivocally that "the (woman) writer who imagines herself assimilated into the mainstream of literature, the literature of men, is surely mistaken, given the evidence of centuries, and the ongoing, by now perplexing, indifference of male critics to female effort. . . . Power does not reside with women—no more in the literary world than in the world of politics and finance—and power is never under the obligation to act justly. A writer may be afflicted by any number of demons, real or imagined, but only the (woman) writer is afflicted by her own essential identity" ("Woman," 30, 31–32). How to deal with this hard truth? "With resilience, with a sense of humor, with stubbornness, with anger, with hope," says Joyce Carol Oates. The "ghetto" is, after all, a place to live.

Oates's work of the last decade is written from this "ghetto," exploring with incisive scrutiny her heritage as a woman and as a woman writer. In a powerful and provocative essay, "At Least I Have Made a Woman of Her," she focuses a critical eye on the deeply misogynistic and sterotypical views of women implicit in our literary and cultural heritage. She finds modernist literature, despite its sophistication in other respects, to exhibit "nonetheless most of the received and unexamined values of popular mass culture, so far as images of Woman are concerned; it is not an exaggeration to argue that Modernist fiction carries over deep-rooted nineteenth-century prejudices of a distinctly bourgeois sort" ("At Least," 35).

In the previous chapter we have seen how some of her most interesting and imaginative fictional works are critical examinations of those deep-rooted nineteenth century prejudices. In fact, in these postmodernist, pro-feminist remimaginings of nineteenth century genres, Oates playfully works out strategies of female escape and liberation which find their way into her subsequent realistic novels, such as the three discussed in this chapter.

Solstice

Solstice (1986), Oates's sixteenth novel, is a study of the dialectics of female friendship, female selfhood, and female creativity. The novel centers on the intense relationship of Monica Jensen, newly hired English instructor at Glenkill Academy for Boys in rural Pennsylvania, and Sheila Trask, a beautiful, eccentric artist and widow a few years older than Monica who lives on a country estate in the vicinity. Filtered through the consciousness of Monica, this short, tautly written novel has a narrowness of focus and a sty-listic restraint that make it quite unlike the spacious, richly imagined, eru-ditely embellished, intricately structured, floridly written novels that preceded it, but it harks back in characterization and theme to *Unholy Loves*. Like Brigit Stott in that earlier novel, Monica is another of Oates's rare por-traits of intelligent professional women.

Scarred both emotionally and physically by a marriage that had recently ended with an abortion, bitter acrimony, and divorce, Monica cautiously at-tempts to shore up her self through a new life and a new identity: "her ear-lier life, her earlier preoccupations, had been wonderfully blotted out."[3] The "Hour of Lead," "the old, old eclipse of the soul," is signaled by the Emily Dickinson poem that serves as epigraph ("After great pain, a formal feeling comes"). Monica tries to cope with her pain by reducing life to an uncompli-cated routine of work and rest. The book is in part a study of the problema-tics of selfhood: To what degree is identity merely a matter of the roles one plays, the labels and titles affixed by others, a life in two dimensions, with-out depth? Many years ago Monica "had been a golden girl of sorts," then Monica Bell, someone's wife, and now Miss Jensen of Glenkill Academy—

who, she hopes, is attractively reflected in the eyes of her students and colleagues.

Sharing a sisterhood with other women with weak egos in Oates's canon, such as Maureen Wendall in *them,* Elena in *Do With Me What You Will,* and Laney in *Childwold,* Monica is similarly intimidated and overpowered by the more assertive self of a much different kind of woman. Only in the earlier books that woman—Loretta, Ardis, Arlene—is the mother; here she is Monica's passionate friend, Sheila, and importantly, she is an artist. Like *Unholy Loves,* the novel *Solstice* is about the complex emotions of both erotic attraction and artistic creation.

Sheila and Monica are opposites—dark and light, willful and passive, stormy and quiescent, mannish and feminine, earthy and intellectual, visual and verbal. The novel details the subtle and sometimes surprising shifts of control and submission, dependency and dominance between them. They struggle to arrive at a solstice, an equilibrium, in a bond both visceral and quixotic. That one woman is an artist, the other a teacher—dual aspects of their creator—is significant. As in her experimental works, Oates's sophisticated use of the double enriches and gives texture to what is otherwise a realistic novel. The double, for Oates, often functions as an alter ego, embodying unfulfilled contexts of the self to which one is both attracted and repelled—a bond that seems at once potentially liberating and potentially annihilating. Monica and Sheila find themselves locked in what is indeed a life-and-death struggle for ascendancy, control, and, ideally, balance: "It was Monica's task, Monica's privilege, to help Sheila maintain an emotional equilibrium: an activity that took a great deal of her time and was in itself exhilarating. Walking a tightrope, high above the ground. Eyes fixed resolutely ahead, arms outspread for balance. The trick being not to look down; not ever to look down" (*S,* 185).

Overtly heterosexual, both women carefully avoid physical contact with one another: "They were shy of touching each other, even of drawing close by accident. Monica recalled that hissed admonition of Sheila's—*I don't care to be touched*—and stiffened, herself, if, in one of her more effusive states, Sheila drew too close. She was conscious of Sheila's warm breath, Sheila's scent" (*S,* 176). Yet one feels that men in the novel are either irrelevant or surrogates who express the compelling attraction and tension between the women. In this portrayal of the relationship of two women, Oates fulfills the hope expressed by Virginia Woolf in *A Room of One's Own* that one day in literature honest, complexly nuanced versions of "Chloe likes Olivia" would be expressed.[4] In the unrelenting focus on erotic tension and obsession—unacknowledged, unexpressed, and unrelieved—*Solstice* is reminiscent of some of D. H. Lawrence's finer short stories. The novel is also about the tension and obsession of artistic creation. Sheila's work, a series of paintings, is called Ariadne's thread. It is said to be about "the labyrinth as a state of mind, a region of the soul: heroic effort without any Hero at its center. ('This is only about Ariadne's thread, this has nothing to do with Theseus,' Sheila said angrily)" (*S*, 53). It is, in other words, about the female weaver-artist without a male savior. It is also about a plunge into the unconscious, into what Sheila calls mind, a labyrinthine territory not controlled by the ego. Monica notes about Sheila's paintings, "All that was significant about them was interior, secret, indefinable; they possessed their own integrity; they *were*. Monica began to understand her friend's almost fanatical interest in technique since 'idea' could only be embodied by way of technique; . . . It was a place where language did not determine action. It was a place, Monica sometimes thought, prior to language. To enter it—to dare to enter it—was to surrender the power of words, and to submit to another sort of power altogether" (*S*, 204).

Through her relationship with Sheila, Monica—herself always associated with light and consciousness and two dimensions ("blond, healthy, forthright. A daylight personality" [*S*, 257]—reaches into this darker side of experience: "Ariadne's thread held tightfully, prayerfully, in the fingers. The labyrinth as a state of mind, a permanent state of mind. Monica wander[s] in it, utterly content" (*S*, 55). She dreams "of the most extraordinary painting, fluid, three-dimensional, throbbing with life: Sheila's painting, perhaps, but only partly imagined, still in the process of being transcribed. Monica was staring at the painting yet at the same time she was in it; swimming in its sweet radiant warmth, in its fleshly-sweet erotic warmth; scarcely daring to breathe because the sensation was so exquisite, so precarious, so forbidding" (*S*, 201). Obvious from this passage are the compelling homoerotic attractions of Sheila, of her passionate nature, of her art, of the dangerous but enticing forces that inspire her vision and infuse her nature.

The relationship is indeed dangerous because power and strength seem to flow from one of the characters into the other and vice versa. The changing nature of the seasons, particularly the "malaise of relentlessly darkening days and relentlessly lengthening nights," parallels the kind of gradual tipping of balance and control between the women. Monica's friend Keith warns her that friendship with a suicidal person "is a cul-de-sac—a kind of maze or labyrinth. Strength seems to flow from the healthy person to the unhealthy but it drains away, it doesn't do the slightest amount of good, it's a profitless situation all around" (*S*, 146). Sheila does in fact sink into a suicidal pattern, and Monica takes control, as the (excessively repetitive) language makes clear:

> Nothing had changed, Monica thought,—except my control.
> For this meant, this time, to be in control.
> She was already, was she not?—in control.
> Yes: in control.
> Control.
> She quite liked the word, its classy air.
> Control. *Control.*
> "This time," she said, "—mine." (*S*, 170)

But Monica's attention to Sheila drains energy and order from her own life. When Sheila seems to be on her way to recovery, Monica herself becomes deathly ill. At the end of the book she is discovered and saved by Sheila, who assertively assumes control: "'You shouldn't have done this—you shouldn't have doubted me—we'll be friends for a long, long time,' she says, 'unless one of us dies'" (*S*, 243).

The novel is a powerful portrayal of the dynamics of a symbiotic relationship that can be read as a commentary on both two-women relationships and the two sides of the female self. Nancy Chodorow, in her seminal feminist revision of Freud, argues that because girls retain an ambivalent gender attachment to their mothers, they experience a "relational complexity in feminine self-definition and personality" not characteristic of males. Girls "come to experience themselves as less separate than boys, as having more permeable ego boundaries"; therefore, adult female friendships "are a way of resolving and recreating the mother-daughter bond and are an expression of women's general relational capacities and definition of self in relationship."[5] Sheila and Monica's relationship demonstrates both women's permeable ego boundaries and their experience of self-in-relationship.

The two women play for a while at being other selves, "Sherrill Ann" and "Mary Beth," working-class tarts who frequent bars and taverns and who flirt "innocently" with men (although after a certain incident Monica, repulsed by this dangerous role-playing, refuses to accompany Sheila). Within the self, moreover, are haunting older sisters, "mirror-leeches" (*S*, 107), portents of the older, aged self. Keeping hold of a secure sense of self is problematic. Monica suffers from her relationship with Sheila, but she dreads her life without this connection to depth: "And if the world's secret panels slid shut? and all became slick shadowless surface? and there remained no texture, no resistance? and she could not bring herself to mourn? and her life was a matter of going on—and on—and on?" (*S*, 147). Because the novel's point of view is restricted exclusively to a third-person summary of Monica's reflections, and because Monica is both self-absorbed and obsessed with Sheila, no other character takes on credible life. Moreover, Sheila remains for both Monica and the reader a matter of texture and surfaces, a composite of qualities rather than a person fully realized in her own right: she is obtrusive, flamboyant, mercurial, slatternly; she is alternatively loving and derisive, monomaniacally driven by her work and self-destructively dissipated. Nonetheless, *Solstice* is a deftly sketched, highly readable little novel, important for its contribution to Oates's probing portrayal of women's consciousness and of their merged, symbiotic relationships to one another.

Marya: A Life

Marya: A Life (1986) is, Oates says, "the most 'personal' of my novels . . . though it is not, in the strictest sense, autobiographical. It contains some autobiographical material, particularly in its opening sections, and it is set, for the most part, in places identical with or closely resembling places I have lived" (Preface to M, 376). In writing the book she returned to her childhood home in upper New York State to "look around." Set in the world that Oates knows so well and portrays so successfully, the novel is told in memorable vignettes, from the night Marya Knauer is awakened by her mother and dragged uncomprehendingly to the morgue to identify the body of her father, killed in a tavern brawl, to the moment when she's grown and receives a letter from her long-lost mother, who had abandoned her and her brothers shortly after their father's death. Oates claims that the book was "a kind of amalgam of events from my mother's life, some events from my own life, and perhaps some events that I heard about when I was growing up. . . . It was my mother's father who was murdered. . . . There are gloomings of real people in the book . . . things in it that are palpable . . . I could say when it happened and where I was and what I was wearing." While drawing closely from her childhood experiences, Oates takes pains to say that "Marya is not really me. Marya is much tougher than I am. I'm not as basically angry as Marya, and I wasn't an orphan . . . Marya is what I would have been . . . I never had to deal with life in such a raw manner as Marya did."[6]

Marya is indeed tough and angry: she is also intelligent, talented, and willful. She creates herself between the moment of abandonment with which the novel begins and the moment of incipient reclamation with which it ends. "What is most autobiographical about the novel," says Oates, "is its inner kernel of emotion—Marya's half-conscious and often despairing quest for her own elusive self" (Preface to *M*, 377). Both through the Jamesian epigraph to the volume ("My first act of freedom will be to believe in freedom") and in her preface, Oates stresses that "the spirit of William James, our greatest American philosopher, pervades Marya's story." Marya, says Oates, is an example of James's "philosophy of the individual, stubborn, self-reliant, ultimately mysterious. The democratic 'pluralistic' universe of which James wrote in such startlingly contemporary terms is one in which old traditions and standards of morality are judged largely useless unless they can be regenerated in uniquely individual terms. This is of course Marya Knauer's universe, in which one forges one's own soul, for better or worse" (Preface to *M*, 378).

The novel is essentially a portrait of the artist as a young woman, tracing the adolescence and early adulthood of a girl of inauspicious beginnings who willfully transforms herself from a tough, foul-mouthed, smart-aleck adolescent into a cool and competent student, professor, writer, and journalist. "Don't you start crying," her mother had warned her, because "once you get started you won't be able to stop."[7] It is advice Marya takes to heart; her life is a progressive steeling of emotions, a strengthening of brittle self-sufficiency, a closing out of feeling through denial and repression, a rejection of the inner world of emotion, softness, and femaleness for the outer, analytical, hard, masculine world of success.

She has intermittent and inchoate recollections of viewing her father's body, but she does not allow herself openly to confront this experience. Living with her aunt and uncle, her cousins, and her two brothers, she is given no straightforward information about her father's death or her mother's disappearance: "These were the years of secret glances exchanged over Marya's head. Of mysterious allusions and hints. 'The trouble,' it was sometimes called, 'the bad luck'" (*M*, 16). When her father's demise is discussed, "Marya learn[s] not to get upset when she overhear[s]. Eventually she learn[s] not even to hear" (*M*, 33). Like other Oatesian characters, she perfects the art of withdrawal, absenting herself mentally from her body: "She slipped away, she was there but not there, *not there* became a place familiar to her. . . . She could be *not there* yet fully present to the others, even listening to what they told her" (*M*, 24).

When she is 8 and her 12-year-old cousin Lee "practices" sexual intercourse with her and masturbates against her, she "[goes] into stone" and says nothing. Through such tactics she survives, but her survival is at considerable emotional expense. She is not a victim, however; she always exacts her revenge. Almost unconsciously, years after her cousin's abuse of her, she knocks down the jack holding the car up over her cousin Lee: "*How do you like it now pig pig pig pig pig*" (*M*, 43), she thinks. Lurking in her subconscious is a dark double, her mother, who had often said to her, "You're just the same as me—*I* know you!" (*M*, 8). She fears she may metamorphose into her mother: "She was terrified of examining her face too closely in the mirror for fear of seeding something forbidden: her mother's face, that slack-lidded wink, the glassy stare, the smile rimmed with lipstick and saliva. And that low jeering murmur—Marya you know who you are, Marya you can't lie to *me*" (*M*, 57).

School is the beginning of Marya's gradual liberation from the limitations of her origins, through the help of male mentors. Her eccentric eighth-grade teacher, Mr. Schwilk, recognizes her intelligence and her ability "to understand, and to register with a smirk or a surprised little laugh, his allusions and his fanciful asides. 'Dear Marya!,' he said once, after class, blinking at her. 'It would be so lonely here without you!'" (*M*, 60). Yet Marya is very conflicted in her allegiance. Mr. Schwilk, after all, is an object of ridicule, and she shares in the cruel jokes and jeering aimed at him. She is bitterly contemptuous of his initial attitude toward the students: "He thinks we matter: doesn't he know?" (*M*, 49). On composition assignments, she risks writing florid stories. Bewildered, he can only comment, "You have a most *feverish* imagination." She learns not to expose this side of her nature. She is hardened in her proud autonomy: "Don't give in, Marya counseled herself. Once you start crying you won't be able to stop" (*M*, 59). Finally, the victim of relentless persecution, Mr. Schwilk collapses of strain, overwork, and exhaustion and leaves the school. But it is learned later that he had turned over his salary for the remainder of the year so a poetry prize could be instituted in his name. Marya wins the first of the annual Brandon P. Schwilk Poetry Awards for a poem she writes in his memory. She wins a scroll, a book of poetry, and a check for $35. In leafing through the poetry anthology she "felt a sensation of excitement mixed with cold sick dread: Had her silly little well-intentioned poem announced, as if by accident, her wish to compete *here?*" (*M*, 70). The life of a writer begins to seem an elusive possibility.

Helping to define that possibility is another mentor of Marya in these early years, Father Clifford Shearing, a dying priest who inspires in her a spate of devotional Catholicism. Assisting him in his scholarly work, Marya is introduced to the fascinating world of "masculine" argument: "To be able to write so well, to wield such a vocabulary; to *argue* so powerfully; to ferret

out miscalculations in a rival's thesis to a mere hair's-breadth of a degree
. . . she wonders if it is an entirely masculine skill, an art of combat by the
way of language, forever beyond *her*" (*M,* 95).

Class valedictorian and recipient of scholarships to the state university,
Marya steadily dates Emmett Schroeder, who begins to talk of getting married. In response to Emmett's advances "she told herself, All right. And
tried not to resist. Except to stiffen involuntarily as she always did . . . I love
you, Emmett I love you, though a part of her mind wanted to rear away and
laugh contemptuously: Why are you doing this? Who do you think you're
deceiving?" (*M,* 109). Emmett is not deceived; shortly before she leaves for
college, their relationship is broken.

Marya is boastful, vain, sarcastic, theatrical, experimentally flirtatious,
daringly provocative, flinging back dirty words at crude boys: "Being *good,*
Marya thought, wasn't a problem she had to worry about." She finds her
feelings for boys and men to be "largely a matter of daydreaming. If she
fastened upon a boy in school he was never so interesting in person as he
seemed in her head, in her wild, floundering imagination." She has no interest in really falling in love, which strikes her as "supremely weak": "While
she assuredly didn't want to be good, or nice, or sweet, or ladylike, her repugnance for any display of weakness was equally strong" (*M,* 113, 114).
Her childhood world is terminated at a crude, drunken, and disastrous
graduation party that ends with her violently fighting an attack by a group
of jeering boys who try to rape her and who succeed in cutting off her long
hair. Symbolically unsexed, she leaves for college declaring herself
"inviolable—autonomous—entirely self-sufficient" (*M,* 207).

A new beginning, life at the university allows her to escape into the pleasures of the life of the mind: "A writer's authentic self, she thought, lay in his
writing and not in his life; it was the landscape of the imagination that en-
dured, that was really real. Mere life was the husk, the actor's performance,
negligible in the long run. . . . How could it be anything more than the ve-
hicle by which certain works of art were transcribed . . . she thought her
happiness almost too exquisite to be borne" (*M,* 135). These thoughts echo
those of other characters (Kasch and Laney in *Childwold,* Brigit in *Unholy
Loves*) and of the author herself: "most human beings, writers or not, are in
disguise as their outward selves . . . their truest and most valuable selves are
interior" ("Exist," 52). "We live the lives we live in order to produce the art
of which we believe ourselves capable" ("Soul," 177).

But the danger of this kind of self-sufficiency is a growing self-
absorption, a Faustian overreaching: "She wanted only to be best, to be outstanding, to be defined to herself as extraordinary . . . for, apart from being

extraordinary, had she any essence at all?" (*M*, 156). This precarious invest-ment in an identity of autonomy and uniqueness is not unusual in Oates's canon—and usually it cannot be sustained.

Two of Marya's stories are accepted for publication, but she is disturbed by her writing: "Not just the content itself—though the content was often wild, disturbing, unanticipated—but the emotional and psychological strain it involved. She could write all night long, sprawled across her bed, taking notes, drafting out sketches and scenes, narrating a story she seemed to be hearing in a kind of trance; she could write until her hand ached and her eyes filled with tears and she felt that another pulse beat would push her over the brink—into despair, into madness, into sheer extinction" (*M*, 176). Recalling the terror and apprehension felt by Brigit Stott in *Unholy Loves* about the self-annihilating danger of the dream world of the unconscious, Marya tells herself "Give up. Don't risk it. *Don't* risk it . . . the waters will suck you down and close over your head." Again rejecting the inner "female" side of herself, she finds the analytical "male" style of writing "highly con-scious, cerebral, critical, discursive . . . far easier; far less dangerous. She was praised for it lavishly, given the highest grades, the most splendid sort of en-couragement" (*M*, 175–76).

Valuing her success in the academy, Marya treasures her straight-A av-erage. Shocked and mortified to get a B-plus, she goes to see the professor, who discovers he had neglected to read her second blue examination booklet. Although he agrees to change the grade, Marya is full of loathing for his attitude and for what she determines to be his mediocrity; she gets her revenge by fabricating a story about her mother's cancer. As he stum-bles through his apologies, she leaves in triumph, having stolen his ex-pensive Parker pen. Tough and not particularly likable, Marya is an unsentimental young woman determined to succeed, a person who will take what she can get.

Marya's only intense relationship with another woman is with Imogene Skillman, a fellow student at college. An attraction and repulsion of oppo-sites, the friendship of the young women recalls that of Sheila and Monica in *Solstice*. Beautiful, rich, and self-possessed, a sorority girl and theater arts major, Imogene is a campus personality whom Marya had closely observed before being taken up as Imogene's brainy "find." Marya is puzzled, discon-certed, and flattered by Imogene's attentions: "Friendship, Marya specu-lated in her journal, the most enigmatic of all relationships" (*M*, 147). Periodically, she finds the vicissitudes of their relationship too upsetting and pulls away: "Friendship, she wrote—a puzzle that demands too much of the imagination" (*M*, 151). She knows that Imogene has a reputation for being "recklessly improvident with her female friends as with her male friends. . . . Why make the effort, Marya reasons, when all that matters in life is one's personal accomplishment? Work, success, that numbing grade-point average . . . that promise of a future, any future" (*M*, 163). Yet she remains in a kind of love-hate bondage to Imogene, from which Imogene's death would be a welcome release: "If Imogene were dying . . . she wouldn't lift a hand to prevent that death!—so she thought" (*M*, 177). After one bitter exchange between them, Marya exacts her typical revenge: she steals a pair of Imogene's earrings. Her behavior is almost instinctive: "Marya had seen her hand reach out to them but she did not remember *taking* them from the room" (*M*, 180). Immediately, she's get her ears pierced, thinking triumphantly, "No one . . . can keep me from my perfect record" (*M*, 181). Wearing the earrings everywhere, Marya is eventually confronted by Imogene on a street, and the two engage in a bitter and violent struggle. Marya is tough and brutal; striking from the shoulder, she bloodies Imogene's mouth and knocks her down. "You'll be all right, Marya thought, someone will always take care of *you*" (*M*, 183). Marya, in contrast, will always take care of herself. Her academic record and her cold self-sufficiency remain inviolate.

After this point, what has been a taut, focused novel becomes much less so. A series of disjointed episodes sketch out the adulthood of Marya Knauer. The first, during Marya's graduate-school days, is her affair with a married mentor, Professor Fein. This is her first sexual relationship: "She supposed she had remained a virgin so long because she hadn't exactly believed in other people—in men. In what they might bring to her that she didn't already possess, in the most secret inchoate depths of her being" (*M*, 208). Marya finds herself split: on the one hand, she goes through the "motions of a daylight life. She was still the good girl, the A-plus student, fired by competition and virtually inexhaustible." On the other hand is her nighttime life, in which her obsession with Fein reigns. Rather curiously, Fein claims "to descend periodically . . . into the Underworld, the Night World; but not by choice. It [is] a species of hell contained within the perimeters of his skull—or, if you like, his soul" (*M*, 201). The night before Marya gets a call from Mrs. Fein, who tells her that the professor lies in a coma, dying, she experiences what seems to be a kind of dream vision of madness: "*Marya, dear Marya, we have come to make our claim.* . . . Suddenly a hot little demon did a jig on her belly digging in his heels. *Hey nonny nonny hey nonny nonny d'you love me Marya will you kiss me Marya . . . !* . . . Marya knew suddenly that this was madness, this was death. This was extinction" (*M*, 229). This seems to be the descent into the underworld, the unconscious, that Marya has always feared, and it is with some difficulty that she shakes herself into consciousness. She retains the hold on her daytime analytical self.

The novel then jumps to an incident in which Marya is taunted by a black janitor in the college at which she teaches. He steals things from her office, rearranges her possessions, uses her toilet. She is exasperated and powerless against him. He functions, apparently, as the black shadow, the dark double, the recurrent reminder of the underside and the fragility of her daytime success.

The next episode is a bicycle trip taken by Marya and a colleague to distract themselves from the tenure and promotion reviews going on at the college. Marya has a strong case, having published a well-received scholarly book, and articles and reviews in her field, and having the reputation of being a dedicated and exacting teacher. She has learned how to succeed within the standards defined by the academy and to keep well hidden the inner, "female," creative part of herself: "She had become shrewd enough to say nothing at all about her nonacademic writing, or to allude to it in the slightly disparaging way in which such writing is generally alluded to, in her profession" (M, 259). The bicycle trip goes poorly, but apparently Marya triumphs again. We learn that she gets tenure and that her male companion does not, and that she later resigns her academic position to become a professional journalist and writer.

In the penultimate episode of the book, Marya, age 34, attends an international conference while mourning the accidental death of her married lover, distinguished editor and journalist Eric Nichols. Even after his death, she acts according to his concerns, listening to his voice, attempting to speak for him. But she breaks down, unable to carry on without her lover as a reference point.

Being very American in her belief in the efficacy of action, Marya reverses the existential premise: "What one *is* follows directly from what one *does*." Yet she finds herself increasingly despondent, not "herself": "The very question of 'self' intrigued her. (For if she could raise her emotional confusion to a philosophical plane, might she not be redeemed? It was an old, old tradition.)" But she has difficulty transforming her malaise into a philosophical or intellectual issue; it seems physiological. Contrary to medical evidence, she feels a "tiny thing" growing in her womb: "But she ignore[s] it. She ignore[s] all notions that [do] not correspond to her knowledge of herself" (M, 293, 294). Nonetheless, the "child" of her unrealized self is struggling to be born. Her experience is partly grief for her dead lover; it is also a realization of the dead end, the emptiness, of the life and the course she has set for herself. In the final chapter she attempts to chart a new direction, back toward the world she has rejected and the mother who rejected her.

While Marya had earlier thought of her mother only "in weak moods, when she clearly wasn't herself," she becomes in the final chapter of the novel obsessed with finding her mother. She places ads in the paper. She goes back to Innisfail to visit her father's grave and to see her relatives. She learns from her aunt Wilma where she might find her mother, and later she writes to her. At the very end of the novel she is just opening her mother's letter of reply: "Marya, this is going to change your life, she thought, half in dread. Marya, this is going to cut your life in two" (*M*, 310).

Oates has commented on how difficult this book was to write—that she could not approach it "head on. I had to write it in self-contained sections." She says that only when she wrote that final sentence did she "fully understand Marya's story, and was then in a position to begin again and to recast it as a single work of prose fiction" (Preface to *M*, 377).

Oates's understanding of Marya perhaps exceeds the reader's. The novel trails off at the end without providing a clear final portrait of Marya. In the preface Oates suggests that Marya "chooses finally not to accept the terms of . . . [her] betrayal" (Preface to *M*, 378). Throughout the novel Oates sympathetically but incisively and unsentimentally judges that betrayal. Yet the end is unresolved, open. To be sure, the implication is certainly that Marya is attempting reintegration with the suppressed "female" side of her being. Perhaps she will somehow integrate feeling and thinking, daytime and nighttime, accomplishment and being, past and present by coming to terms with her lost mother and with the community of women.[8] Oates is always most effective when she portrays primal bonds. One wishes that she had done so in this novel instead of terminating the story at the moment of climax.

You Must Remember This

You Must Remember This (1987) is yet another retrospective look at the past for Joyce Carol Oates. It too is set in the familiar upper New York State milieu of her childhood. Recalling earlier Oatesian family sagas, the novel portrays the period 1953–56 in the lives of the Stevick family, who live in a rented duplex near the U.S. Steel and Swale Cyanamid factories in Port Oriskany, a fictitious city based loosely on Oates's hometown of Lockport. *You Must Remember This* is a thickly textured novel by an author who well remembers, and successfully evokes, the ambience and events of that time: the popular songs (including "As Time Goes By" of *Casablanca* fame, from which the book's title is taken), the familiar programs of early television, the political campaigns of Adlai Stevenson and Dwight Eisenhower, the executions of the Rosenbergs, the cold war aftermath of the Korean conflict, the Red hysteria stirred up by Senator McCarthy, the preoccupation with civil defense.

The father of the family, Lyle, is a used-furniture dealer; the mother, Hannah, is a harassed mother and housewife. The four children have set off on different paths: for Geraldine, quick marriage and motherhood; for Lizzie, a sleazy singing career; for Warren, disfigured in the Korean War, the life of a crusading pacifist; and for Enid, an honors student of great promise, a clandestine affair with her half-uncle Felix.

Enid and Felix are the central characters and the affair the central tension of the novel. In fact, the novel begins in medias res with a flash forward to the moment on June 7, 1953, when the 15-year-old Enid "happily" attempts suicide by swallowing a bottle of aspirin. She does this, we learn later, in response to her Uncle Felix's attempt to break off their relationship after having seduced her one night in a drunken, excited state. Their relationship becomes a study of the dialectics of passion and control. It grows out of and is nurtured by inner conflicts and dualities within the two characters. As is so often the case in Oates's work, a sexual relationship is an acting out of the attraction to and repulsion from the other, an external manifestation of dualities implicit in one's own nature and, indeed, in human nature.

Enid is a poignant study of the emotional vicissitudes and the inchoate sense of self that characterize adolescence, a period of life that Oates is particularly skillful at rendering. Enid's sense of being "double" and "duplicitous" extends to her having two names for the two sides of her nature. "Enid Maria" is her "good" side, the reliable A student, the talented musician, the dutiful daughter, the devout Catholic. "Angel-face," on the other hand, is "Enid too but sly wriggly hot-skinned treacherous, with eyes like delicious chocolate candies and an innocent watchful expression, delicate-boned as a bird . . . and sneaky. . . . Enid Maria knew very little about Angel-face while Angel-face knew everything about Enid Maria."[9] Angel-face introduces disorder, chaos, excitement into Enid Maria's life: scrambling her bureau drawers, losing her library books or lunch money, jaywalking, engaging in petty theft. Running out of a store after a shoplifting spree, she thinks, "Oh sweet Jesus, Angel-face could run forever she would live forever nobody dared touch her" (*Y*, 42).

There is yet another side of Enid, a side that believes she will not "live forever" but will be overcome by Death. She fights a volitionless death wish. She stands mesmerized on a railroad track with the train coming. She finds it hard to walk on a bridge because "if she could see the water below that was the danger, the tug the pull the impulse to climb over the railing and fall, drown; she must take care never to be guided by a will external to her own" (*Y,* 87). She thinks of the "Death-panic" as being "not the desire to die but her resistance to that desire. When she died she would die by her own hand, she vowed, by her own choice, she would not give in to the urgings of a will external to her own even if the will was God's. *She would not*" (*Y,* 87–88).

This is a book very much about control, and it is no wonder. Enid is born into a tough, dangerous world of gratuitous violence in seedy Port Oriskany. A recurrent image in Enid's consciousness is that of an incident she observed in her childhood: some boys caught a mourning dove, sprinkled it with gasoline, and set it afire. "The bird flew up, its wings flapping, it turned in circles, shrieking, ablaze, then suddenly it gave up, and fell straight down to the ground just a patch of burning feathers" (*Y,* 12). Enid identifies with the dove, fearing that she too will have her flight, her freedom, cruelly aborted. Nonetheless, one side of her is daring, wild.

In her Angel-face mode she engages in a dangerous flirtation with her Uncle Felix, playing hide-and-seek in an empty resort inn, ending up in his crudely impersonal muscular embrace: "He seemed hardly aware of her except as a presence, a body giving him some small unwitting resistance, his will was dominant, all-obliterating. Enid understood that he was detached from her and from the rather anguished mechanical act he had performed, even as he stood swaying drunken against her, his arm crooked around her neck locking her in place, his hot shamed face in her hair, still he was somehow separate from her, saying her name, her name, so sweet so sweet so sweet—he swallowed a belch and Enid smelled beer" (*Y,* 118). After the incident the love-struck adolescent is obsessed with her uncle: she writes him a note saying "*Felix I want to die. I love you so much*" (*Y,* 120).

Deeply regretting the incident and urging her not to tell anyone about it, Felix is determined to keep away from Enid. One day, seeing her hitchhiking, he picks her up in his car and lectures her on the dangers of her behavior, the foolishness of her note to him, and his remorse about what had happened at the lake ("I'm sorry for what happened Jesus Christ I'm disgusted I'm not that kind of shit really!—taking advantage of a girl your age my own brother's daughter I'm not that kind of man" [*Y,* 132]). Finally, exasperated, he slaps the side of her face: "She hadn't seen it coming and her head knocked against the window for an instant she was stunned, astonished." Feeling rejected, out of control, a victim of life's unexpected blows, she feels this blow to be the sign she had been waiting for, the sign that now is the time to take "control"—to choose death deliberately.

Such an attitude toward death is common in Enid's family. Her Grandfather Stevick, dying of cancer in a hospital bed, had shot himself in order
"to take control of his dying. Yes, that was it, Enid thought. Control" (*Y*,
124). Her father takes comfort in the suicide rope he has stashed in the
basement of his store.

Now Enid tries "happily," willfully, to commit suicide. Her Uncle Felix sees
the act for what it is: an attempt to manipulate him, to take control away
from him. A former boxer, he sees the two of them bonded now, locked in a
fighting match: "He didn't love her but there was this connection between
them now, this bond. A blood bond as if between two men who'd fought
each other to a draw. Or say one of them beat the other decisively but the losing fighter fought a courageous fight and pushed himself beyond his limit—
the winner was forever in his debt. Yes, she'd had her way" (*Y*, 168).

Felix must be seen within the boxing context that has indelibly shaped
his being and his attitude toward life. As a boy he "thrived on opposition,
resistance" (*Y*, 165). He took all his heroes "directly from the boxing world,"
which seemed "far more significant" than the real world. He is taken with
the accountability and intentionality of the boxing world: "if you're hit it's
because you deserve to be hit, meaning you aren't able to defend yourself
against your opponent, meaning you should never have entered the ring
with him, meaning you deserve all that happens to you even death—
nothing is accidental. He saw nothing like it anywhere else in the world" (*Y*,
166). He has a boxing career of great promise until he makes the mistake of
losing control, of "getting angry with his opponent getting emotional trad-
ing punches standing toe to toe 'man to man'" (*Y*, 166). He loses his sense
of invincibility, invulnerability; he loses his unguarded joy in the body. He
experiences instead the punch he "hadn't seen coming. . . . He'd seen his
death like an opening, an entranceway, hazy with light, but chill. He saw it
and tasted it" (*Y*, 167). It is the awareness that he could experience the blow
he "hadn't seen coming" and could die that ends his boxing career.

Through a young protege, Jo-Jo, Felix experiences again, vicariously, the
ecstasy of life in the flesh, which boxing epitomizes: "It was ecstasy, it was
oblivion, the joy of the body as Felix Stevick had once known it before he'd
been made to realize that he was going to die" (*Y*, 233). Even though he experiences the reality of death when Jo-Jo is battered so badly he dies, Felix
finds ordinary life a pale imitation of "life speeded up" in the ring.

His life is deliberately one-dimensional; he attempts to live on a purely instinctual level. "Felix [is] not a reflective man—he [doesn't] give a good deal
of conscious thought to anything, just trust[s] his instincts" (*Y*, 235). He believes in doing what gives pleasure. When Enid asks him why boxers fight, he

responds simply, "Why fuck?—it feels good" (*Y,* 229). After her attempted suicide, they pursue what feels good in an intensely passionate affair, which they both experience as a kind of trancelike obsession, "a languorous blood-heavy extinction of their minds. She saw he was angry with her, he was sick with desire for her, the rest of the world was distant, obliterated. Enid felt a shuddering sensation of the kind she had felt sinking into sleep, into Death" (*Y,* 181). Now she craves not real death but orgasm, the "little death" of Renaissance literature. She realizes it was only Enid Maria she had wanted to kill—the omnipresence of ego consciousness—not her life itself. Now through sexuality she feels herself to be more fully connected to instinctual life and is terrified at the thought of either herself or Felix dying.

For a time the relationship gives her a sense that "she [is] happy . . . in perfect equilibrium, her two selves perfectly balanced" (*Y,* 222). She experiences a sense of connection to the world, which allows her to grow and develop in other facets of her life:

> She was in love and her love set her in a relationship with the world that was unexpected, potent, mysterious. Because of Felix she had the power to cultivate friendships where she wished, she had the power to cultivate her own quick restless analytical intelligence as if it were a factor distinct from her own personality. She gave herself up to hours of piano practice, grateful for the sensation of fatigue when she stopped—a head-swimming fatigue like that following love. Thinking of Felix, of when they'd last been together and when they would next meet, she felt her senses sharpened and dilated almost to the point of pain. Suddenly everything was vivid, piercing, tremulous with meaning. (*Y,* 225)

Yet the romance has its dark underside. This is, after all, a clandestine, incestuous relationship with an uncle twice her age. He tries, and succeeds to a certain degree, to keep her compartmentalized in his life: "he needed Enid set off in some private space he could enter when he wanted, it was a compartment in his mind like memory" (*Y,* 235).

Felix's urgent sexual needs take precedence, intruding carelessly, dangerously into Enid's "good girl" school life. Enid must be loosened up with wine or alcohol before sex. In her more sober moments she questions whether they are locked together in love or in sickness: "Enid didn't know even now whether she loved him or he loved her or whether their feeling for each other was a sickness lodged deep inside them that others would see at once was a sickness and recoil in disgust" (*Y,* 379). Her thoughts recall Joyce Carol Oates's on D. H. Lawrence's deeply ambivalent attitudes toward sexual love: Is it "an ecstatic experience" or "a delusion"? Is erotic love "salvation" or "a distraction, a burden? . . . Is it something to be gone through in order that one's deepest self may be stirred to life? Or is it a very simple, utterly natural emotion?"[10] What is almost shocking about the novel is its relentless honesty in portraying both the highs and the lows of obsessive sexual passion. The two characters are within the grips of a passion that at times overwhelms them. They are not judged harshly, even though their incestuous affair grows increasingly sordid.

As their passion ebbs, Enid sees more clearly the limitations of her uncle, the emptiness of his life. She is made especially aware of this by the unlived-in quality of his apartment: "Enid had a sudden flash of her uncle sitting in this place alone, always alone, drinking black coffee without tasting it, smoking his Camels without tasting them, skimming newspapers finding nothing to engage his interest. He'd told her in his deadpan faintly bemused way that there was nothing in the world—in the larger world—that caught him up, excited him, made him angry or hopeful or disgusted or disappointed: what would it be?" (Y, 390). In the war, his "deepest self, his soul, had never been involved as it had been involved in the least of his amateur boxing matches." He has no political beliefs beyond what he wants for himself. She thinks of him as cynical and wishes not to be cynical herself. Looking at him coldly, she feels "overcome by a sense of despair, sorrow. She [can't] bear to look at Felix any longer: it [is] as if a part of herself [stands] before her, her own being in Felix, so *useless,* so *without purpose,* doomed" (Y, 392).

The lowest of the lows is Enid's realization that she is pregnant and will have to undergo an abortion. She dreams recurrently of the singed "dove flying upward in wild widening fiery circles out of her vision" (Y, 370). The love between Enid and Felix does end in death after all, a death that effects a permanent separation between them. Felix, deeply upset, takes out his displaced anger and guilt by beating up a pimp; then, in a kind of poetic justice, he himself is severely beaten by Jo-Jo's father. We learn later, however, that he recovers and prevails. The last Enid hears of him is that he is getting married and moving out of Port Oriskany.

Similarly, Enid recovers, prevails, and moves on. In the epilogue of the book, she visits the elite music school she will attend as a scholarship recipient in the fall. "Wave upon wave of happiness washed over her. *You don't deserve it,* she knew but she didn't care, she *was* here" (Y, 423). She and Felix should have died, Enid thinks, yet their lives evade the heavy, tragic endings of their movie-screen counterparts. This is a book about survival, about the renewal of the human spirit. Enid is now ready to devote herself to the piano. "She was willing to work, she was willing to humble herself starting over and beginning again, for what after all was the alternative" (*Y,* 424).

Oates's novels, one might argue, have always been about survival. Despite horrific events—violence, brutality, sexual assault—her characters usually carry on in the end, "for what, after all, [is] the alternative?" But survival in this novel is more life-affirming, more optimistic. Why is that?

In Oates's earlier books survival, for female characters in particular, is attained at great cost to emotional and sexual well-being. One thinks of Maureen Wendall in *them,* who turns to prostitution as a way out of poverty, who sinks into a kind of living death of catatonia, who builds a cautious, protective shell around her. Her survival is precarious. Marya, too, who most resembles Enid and faces the same need to go beyond the limitations of her environment, survives by hardening herself, by denying her inner being. While her future is as unknown as Marya's, Enid would appear to have a better chance of success at surviving whole—having gone through sexual initiation without being destroyed, having enjoyed sexuality without being fatally punished, having coped with both the highs and the lows of illicit (indeed, incestuous) sexual passion, having even perhaps integrated the dualities of her being.

She is most like the awakened Elena in *Do With Me What You Will* and that "unregenerate murderess" Perdita in *Mysteries of Winterthurn.* Sexuality and criminality, Oates's work implies, are part of being human for women as well as for men. Girls are more resilient than fictional conventions have portrayed them, Oates seems to argue. In this novel, at least, she does not weigh down the character with heavy psychological or moralistic retribution. "*You don't deserve it,*" Enid thinks, and she is right. She is both victim and criminal. Her behavior has been reprehensible and ugly and wrong. Yet she is also humanly capable of living with her guilt, of continuing to engage with life. Her talent, compassion, intelligence, and hope are the qualities of a survivor, especially when coupled with her Angel-face daring, resilience, irreverence, skepticism, and willfulness.

So too does Enid's family survive and prevail with a kind of normality rare in Oates's fiction. The novel is finally compassionate, forgiving. Another especially resilient character is Warren, Enid's brother, who undergoes body- and mind-fracturing experiences in the Korean War but who is driven by a persistent idealism to be an early antinuclear protestor. This positive characterization contrasts sharply with Oates's earlier disturbing portrait of the disturbed veteran Vale in *Childwold.* The vicissitudes of Warren's emotional and sexual life and of his attachment to his sister are detailed; indeed, there are echoes of the Maureen-Jules relationship in *them.* But the Stevicks, one feels, are stronger survivors, relying less on luck and protective security, and more on education, talent, and inner reserves of strength, to shape their lives. The most interesting survivor is the father, Lyle Stevick. In many ways a fool and a failure, he is nonetheless warmly, humanely rendered. The long passages detailing his rambling thought processes—his incidental lust, his bogus adulterous adventure, his jealousy of his half-brother, his anxieties over his children, his restless puzzling about the meaning of life, his thoughts about books and the literature he had studied, his musing about world events are vivid—reminiscent in some ways of Bloom's thoughts in Joyce's *Ulysses*. Ludicrously, his modest education, intelligence, and reason get him in trouble in the hysterical Red-baiting age in which he lives. Because he tells a customer that the land mass of the U.S.S.R. and the People's Republic of China exceeds that of the United States, he is arrested and charged with "suspected subversion" and "promulgating of Communist propaganda." His store is searched and he is suspiciously eyed for having so many books: "And why did he stock books like the atlas, and all those encyclopedias, the *Britannica* for instance—wasn't that a foreign book—*if he was running a furniture store?*" (*Y,* 74). He gets released, but he is shaken up.

But while critical of Red-baiting, he shares in another hysteria of the cold war, civil defense. He wants to built a bomb shelter in the backyard of his rented home. Borrowing the money from his half-brother Felix, he becomes absorbed in this project; it is his way to protect himself and his family from a hostile and assaulting world, to assert some control over life's unpredictabilities. At the end of the novel he escorts his wife Hannah on an inspection of the quarters and, after years of abstinence and failure, successfully makes love to her in a scene that is comically grotesque and unromantic but also, finally, life- and love-affirming. He triumphs momentarily with a sense of mastery, control, and love.

The novel ends with this passage: "And now it was over. It was over. Lyle Stevick lay spent and panting beside his wife, jammed against the wall, his head bumping the bedframe but he didn't give a damn; his heart still pounding now in triumph, all his veins flushed with surprise and well-being and gratitude, he said, "Thank you, Hannah," he said, "I love you, Hannah," and after a moment came the quiet nearly inaudible reply, "I love you too" (*Y,* 435–36). It is hard to think of another Oates work with this tolerance, this mellow spirit, this acceptance of both the comedy and the tragedy of the ordinary and the human.

Chapter Five
Author and Other

Taken as a child by her father to see boxing matches, Joyce Carol Oates has retained a lifelong fascination with the sport. The expertise and thoughtfulness she brings to the subject are evident in her well-written, aphoristic book *On Boxing* (1987), in the several occasional essays she's written on the topic, and in her fictional portrayals of the sport. The Sweet Art of Bruising elicits a complex array of responses from the author—responses that help to illuminate her thought and her craft, and that help to explain, by analogy, why she is attracted to a pseudonymous other.

On Boxing

For a woman, says Oates, boxing is a study of the other: "boxing is for men, and is about men, and *is* men. A celebration of the lost religion of masculinity all the more trenchant for its being lost." Boxing is a "remnant" of an earlier era "predating civilization . . . before God was love," when "the physical being was primary and the warrior's masculinity its highest expression." The "claustrophobic world" of professional boxing is "a distillation of the masculine world, empty now of women, its fantasies, hopes and stratagems magnified as in a distorting mirror, or a dream" (*OB*, 72, 77, 74).

One part of Oates's response to boxing is fascinated horror and loathing. Hers is the perspective of the other, the mesmerized voyeur, who is implicated in the ugliness and madness that are dramatized: "I feel it as vertigo—breathlessness—a repugnance beyond language: a sheerly physical loathing. That it is also, or even primarily, self-loathing goes without saying" (*OB*, 102). Oates's voyeuristic role in relationship to this sport might be likened to her relationship as a writer to the seamy aspects of our culture. She suggests that a writer's role (and hers in particular) may be to "sanctify the world," to articulate the "very worst" aspects of our culture and civilization so that they can be felt and understood. Similarly, boxing is an image "of mankind's collective aggression; its ongoing historical madness" (*OB*, 21).

Boxing is emblematic of the primitive brutality at the heart of life, a stripped-down version of the Darwinian struggle for survival. It makes "visible what is invisible in us." That "this world is conceived in anger—and in hatred, and in hunger—no less than it is conceived in love: that is one of the things that boxing is about," says Joyce Carol Oates. The primary rule, "to defend oneself at all times—is both a parody and a distillation of life" (OB, 68, 48).

Boxing's paradoxical nature is that its savagery is contained by "its myriad rules, regulations, traditions, and superstitions. It seems to make quotidian that which is uncanny, dangerous, forbidden, and unclean: it ritualizes violence, primarily male violence, to the degree that violence becomes an aesthetic principle."[1]

Likening boxing to the Balinese cockfight, subject of Clifford Geertz's classic anthropological essay "Deep Play," Oates suggests that boxing too is a "species of 'deep play' (an action in which stakes are so high that it is, from a utilitarian standpoint, irrational for men to engage in it at all) that seems to demonstrate the way the world really is and not the way it is said, or wished, or promised to be" ("Blood," 266). Boxing is a ritualized violation of the taboo against violence. Oates draws on Freud's *Totem and Taboo* for her sense of the paradoxical nature of taboo: it is sacred and consecrated at the same time that it is dangerous, uncanny, forbidden, and unclean. What is taboo is the primitive id, the unconscious: "that aspect of us that lies undefined, and inaccessible to consciousness: the core of impersonality within the carefully nurtured and jealously prized 'personality' with which we are identified, by ourselves and others" ("Blood," 264).

As he ceremonially disrobes, the boxer ceases to be an individual "with all that implies of a socially regulated ethical bond with other individuals" ("Blood," 267). He disrobes himself "of both reason and instinct's caution as he prepares to fight" (OB, 108). In the boxing ring, values are reversed; the boxer is valued for being a "killer." Its values are primitive: it is about anger and aggression and impotence. "Impotence takes many forms—one of them being the reckless physical expenditure of physical potency" (OB, 69). It is hierarchal: two men cannot occupy the same space at the same time.

The referee is our "intermediary" in the fight; "he is our moral conscience extracted from us as spectators so that, for the duration of the fight, 'conscience' need not be a factor in our experience; nor need it be a factor in the boxers' behavior" (OB, 47). The kind of frenzied attraction so many men have to boxing has to do not only with the power of taboo to "violate, or transcend or render obsolete conventional categories of morality," but also with boxing's dramatization of the "dark, denied, muted, eclipsed, and whole unarticulated underside of America's religion of success" ("Blood," 265). Boxing is a "reading of American experience, unsentimentalized and graphic." It shows how weak the civilized values, the virtues, "presumably Christian," and "the stratagems (manipulative? *feminine?*) of indirection." Boxing shows that as Rocky Graziano once said, "The fight for survival is the fight" ("Blood," 267).

Oates's horror and loathing of boxing coexists with her respect for both the boxer and his romantic quest for transcendence of self. This sometimes tragic quest has physical, psychological and cultural implications and parallels the quests of Oates's fictional characters—and those of the author herself.

Boxing dramatizes the irrefutable fact of life in the body, in the flesh, just as Oates's fictional works situate human life clearly within the physical. In boxing, life in the flesh is celebrated even as it is "consumed," and "the limitations, sometimes tragic, more often poignant, of the physical" are dramatized (*OB*, 9). Boxing, as ritualized drama, has affinities to tragedy, and the boxer can be likened to a tragic hero.

Like an Aristotelian tragedy, a boxing match is "serious, complete, and of a certain magnitude." It is a ceremonial, contained "story: a unique and highly condensed drama without words. . . . Boxers are there to establish an absolute experience, a public accounting of the outermost limits of their being; they will know, as few of us can know, how much or how little, they are capable" (*OB*, 8). A great boxing match gives to the spectator "something like the mysterious catharsis of which Aristotle wrote, the purging of pity and terror by the exercise of these emotions; the subliminal aftermath of classical tragedy." Sports provides a kind of delirious, inverted substitute for religion, if religion is, as Santayana speculated, "another world to live in." It releases energies that are "demonic by the standards of ordinary—or do I mean noncombative?—life. The triumphant boxer is Satan transmogrified as Christ" ("Blood," 273, 250, 253).

Oates finds in boxing yet another arena for her obsessive fascination with the other, the shadow self, and with the dialectics of emotion and will. Boxing "is the quintessential image of human struggle, masculine or otherwise, against not only other people but one's own divided self" ("Blood," 231). Dramatized in graphically physical terms are the mysterious dynamics of the self: boxers attempt to arrive at "the outermost limits of their beings; they will know, as few of ourselves, what physical and psychic power they possess—of how much, or how little, they are capable." The opponent is a "dream-distortion" of the self (*OB*, 8). The boxer's strengths are mirror opposites of his opponent's weaknesses; the boxer's failure is the opponent's triumph. Boxing is about the triumphant or defeated human will. Nothing happens in the ring that is not a product of the boxer's will or failure of will.

In ordinary experience a single-minded attempt to impose one's will can often become a deluded romanticism, a substitution of the self for the world—but in the self-referential boxing ring the will must be triumphant: this is "sanity turned inside out, 'madness' revealed as a higher and more pragmatic form of sanity." Played out is the "body's dialogue with its shadow-self—or Death." Nothing that happens to the boxer, including his death, "is not of his own will or failure of will. The suggestion is of a world-model in which we are humanly responsible not only for our own acts, but for those performed against us" (*OB*, 15, 18, 13).

It is important to see that Oates does not see boxing as a metaphor for life; rather, it is "a unique, closed, self-referential world, obliquely akin to those of severe religions in which the individual is both 'free' and 'determined'—in one sense possessed of a will tantamount to God's, in another totally helpless. The Puritan sensibility would have understood a mouth filling with blood, an eye popped out of its socket—fit punishment for an instant's negligence" (*OB*, 13).

In this self-referential world the individual does matter: "There as in no other public arena does the individual as a unique physical being assert himself; there, for a dramatic and fleeting period of time, the great world with its moral and political complexities, its terrifying impersonality, ceases to exist" (*OB*, 114). The immortal greats of boxing "are always with us." In this arena time and death can romantically and momentarily be defeated. The appeal of Mike Tyson and his great predecessors, says Oates, "is that, in however artificial and delimited a context, a human being, *one of us,* reduced to the essence of physical strength, skill, and ingenuity, has control of his fate"—if, Oates wryly adds, "this control can manifest itself merely in the battering of another human being into absolute submission" ("Blood," 276).

The successful boxer, often from an impoverished background, often black, can at least for a time, literally as well as symbolically, transcend his fate; he can enact the American dream, make millions of dollars, receive the adulation of a hero. He can also fail. Boxing is as much about failure as about success; it is about being hit as well as about hitting; "it is about feeling pain, if not devastating psychological paralysis, more than it is about winning." It is about having "heart," the courage to face the risks and the blows and not give up.

Fictionally, Oates portrays the failed boxer who experiences the devastating blow that he hadn't seen coming in both *You Must Remember This* (discussed in chapter 4) and in a short story entitled "Golden Gloves" in the collection *Last Days* (1984). In both the short story and the novel the unexpected blow is a daunting reminder of death, which abortively ends a promising career. Echoing Felix's similar thoughts in *You Must Remember This,* the Golden Gloves contender of the short story, knocked out just before his eighteenth birthday, thinks: "it was his own death that had crashed into him—yet no more than he deserved . . . he was hit and he died . . . Something opened, lifted, a space of some kind clearing for him to enter his own death, but he hadn't had the courage to step forward."[2] Both men, like Mike Tyson, think that "other than boxing, everything is so boring" (epigraph to "Blood," 254), yet both lack the heart to face "life speeded up" in the ring again.

In both fictional contexts, Oates contrasts boxing, the quintessential male sport, with childbirth, the quintessential female experience. In *On Boxing* Oates speculates that "men fighting men to determine worth (i.e., masculinity) excludes women as completely as the female experience of childbirth excludes men. And is there, perhaps, some connection?" (*OB,* 72–73). The connection, the short story implies, is that through childbirth a woman, like a boxer, faces incredible pain and risk to reach an exalted, privileged sense of life in the flesh: motherhood. The former boxer tries to explain to his pregnant wife, Annemarie, that "she will be risking something few men can risk, she should know herself exalted, privileged, in a way invulnerable to hurt even if she is very badly hurt, she'll be risking something he himself cannot risk again in his life. And maybe he never risked it at all" ("Gloves," 69).

Childbirth, like boxing, is about life in the body, about resilience, about being able to channel pain and suffering toward a higher end—and about the failure to do so. In *You Must Remember This,* Enid Maria's abortion parallels Felix's aborted boxing career, but neither is the end of the story for these characters. Unlike the failed boxer of the short story, who says to his wife softly after she is asleep, "I'm not sure I'll be here when you come back," both Felix and Enid Maria do eventually learn to live with their momentary failures and defeats.

Not only is boxing, in Oates's thought, likened to giving birth; it is also likened to the art of writing. To box is to choose pain in preference to ordinary life and to transform willfully pain into its polar opposite: "If this is masochism—and I doubt that it is, or that it is simply—it is also intelligence, cunning, strategy. Boxing is an act of consummate self-determination —the constant reestablishment of the parameters of one's being." In this willful transformation of pain and conflict into achievement and triumph, in the "fantastic subordination of the self in terms of a wished-for destiny" (*OB,* 26), the boxer is like the writer, who in a different realm is absorbed with the "fascination of what's difficult," and who also constantly reestablishes the parameters of his or her being in an attempt to transcend its limitations and create a "monument of unaging intellect." The timebound spectacle of the boxing match is analogous to the publication of a writer's book. The public part is but the "final stage in a protracted, arduous, grueling, and frequently despairing period of preparation." The two arts are similar in the discipline, the dedication, the fanaticism, the Faustian overreaching, the terrible price exacted for glory.

On the other hand, the boxer is the mirror opposite of the writer in being "all public display, all risk and, ideally, improvisation . . . [the boxer] will know his limit in a way that the writer, like all artists, never quite knows his limit—for we who write lie in a kaleidoscopic world of ever-shifting assessments and judgments, unable to determine whether it is revelation or supreme self-delusion that fuels our most crucial efforts" (OB, 59).

But there is another parallel: writers, like boxers, "perform" before an audience, responding in complex ways to its "mysterious will." Even in their private lives boxers are not necessarily immune to audience: Oates comments on how boxers, both inside and outside the ring, "frequently display themselves . . . as characters in the literary sense of the word. Extravagant fictions without a structure to contain them" (OB, 52). So too do writers have public personas, which can sometimes be oppressive. People believe they know "Joyce Carol Oates," for example; their preconceptions and judgments about the writer and her work color their responses to her new publications.

Indeed, wanting to be free to experiment with a writerly self independent of "Joyce Carol Oates," the author recently published under the pseudonym Rosamond Smith; as it turned out, however, her true identity was exposed. In using a pseudonym, she follows a long line of famous precursors. She understands the impulse well; in an essay on the subject, "Pseudonymous Selves," she suggests that writers attempt to attain through a pseudonym "an interior and not merely an outward transformation, a conspicuous redefining of the self"[3]—to transcend the limitations of the authorial self. Oates recognizes the deep drive within the human psyche to break through narrow and rigid definitions of the self, to push against the outer parameters of one's being. Her pseudonymous novels are part of that drive to achieve fuller selfhood.

Lives of the Twins

Lives of the Twins (1987), the first book published by Oates under the pseudonym Rosamond Smith, is appropriately about a woman obsessed with the other—the identical twin brother of her lover. This book, like so many others of Oates's, is about the contradictory doubleness within the self. Indeed, Oates suggests that boxing is a nightmare image of that duality: "Boxing as dream-image or nightmare, pits self against self, identical twin against twin, as in the womb itself where 'dominancy,' that most mysterious of human hungers, is first expressed" ("Blood," 265).

The novel depicts the affair of an intelligent but shallow and trendy woman, Molly Marks, with her former psychotherapist, Jonathan. Molly discovers that Jonathan has an estranged identical twin brother, James, also a psychotherapist. She becomes obsessed with learning more about the brother, but Jonathan won't talk. Pretending to be a client, she makes an appointment to see James and quickly becomes involved in a clandestine relationship with him.

Jonathan and James are hauntingly similar in appearance, yet they are strikingly antithetical in nature. Jonathan is the "good" twin: kind, considerate, altruistic, gentle, loving, and idealistic. James is the "bad" twin: cruel, blunt, egotistical, brutal, cold, and cynical. While pretending to be indifferent to each other, the twins know that their lives have been highly interdependent, intertwined.

Molly seems to sense that they continue in some ways to be halves of one whole, and she is driven, without knowing why, toward union with both. She is especially keen to learn about the incident several years earlier that had caused such a decisive rift between the brothers. She learns that as babies they sucked each other's thumbs; as children they scored identically on IQ tests and exams; as adults they were attracted to the same women. Eleven minutes older, James claims to be the "dominant" twin who can, when convenient, read Jonathan's mind and who can also successfully impersonate him.

In fact, the mystery that Molly pursues, and does not uncover until near the end of the book, has to do with an impersonation. Years back, Jonathan had been engaged to Sandra Shearer, his high-school sweetheart. Apparently, James had pretended to be Jonathan and gotten Sandra, a virgin, to make love with him. When Jonathan had discovered this treachery, he had broken his engagement with Sandra and ceased to love her. Distraught, Sandra had attempted to kill herself with a gun and ended up a physically and mentally impaired invalid, cared for by her mother.

Molly feels an affinity with Sandra. Sandra is her "twin": the living embodiment of a recurring dream she has about "a featureless face . . . A living being, a person, a woman no doubt. My twin? Molly wonders."[4] Upon meeting Sandra, Molly thinks: "Her face has the look of a mask carelessly imprinted upon a human face. My nightmare, Molly Marks thinks. Here" (*LT,* 208–9). Sandra had been, like Molly, strikingly pretty. Like Molly, she had been in love with Jonathan. Like Molly, she had gotten involved with James, almost against her will. But Molly senses a deeper similarity. Sandra's identity is as tenuous as Molly's. Sandra, after her accident, had become to all her former acquaintances—except her mother—forgettable. She had been a pretty girl, like many others; she had been a good student, like many others. People have a hard time remembering her: "Yes of course he remembers the girl, seems to remember her, although he could be describing, Molly thinks, any number of girls—honors student, student leader, serious hard-working reliable, in the classic tradition of Wellcome School etcetera. Too many Sandys, thinks Molly. Too many of us" (*LT*, 160). From her own experience, too, Molly learns about "the jarring impersonality of the world, inhabited by men who often looked at her avidly but without recognition." She finds performing to be easier "than being herself (whoever 'herself' is)" (*LT*, 22).

Just as Sandra's mother holds on to an image of the "real" Sandra, Molly has a dream repeatedly that her dead mother is watching her, judging her, that her mother alone is a witness to her life as it really is. Her nightmare vision of her twin supplants that of her mother. Sandra becomes the living replica of Molly. But Sandra is a twin with a difference: like Jonathan to James, she is the "good" obverse of the "bad" Molly.

Whereas Sandra had been a "good" honors student, Molly, who had attended several colleges, had never managed to graduate from any. Whereas Sandra had had a steady job, Molly flits from job to job, "waiting, still, for her life's vocation to declare itself." Whereas Sandra had been a "good" girl, a virgin, Molly "makes no effort to recall the men with whom she was involved, casually or otherwise" (*LT*, 34).

Good or bad, however, the important similarity between the women is their essential anonymity and their dependence on a man, Jonathan, to complete their lives, to make them whole. This is a problematic route to selfhood even under the best of circumstances, and they have the additional misfortune of choosing a man who is himself deeply divided, bound up with his twin. Inadvertently, unwillingly, they are both attracted to, repelled by, and drawn into a relationship with his twin.

At several levels and in several different ways, the novel plays on ideas of the double, duality, duplicity, dividedness. It would not be an overstatement to say that the divided self is the crux—the heart—of Oates's work. *Lives of the Twins* is a stripped-down, highly focused portrayal of that duality, which takes many forms: male and female, reason and passion, light and dark, conscious and unconscious, good and evil, passive and aggressive. Why Sandra and Molly are both drawn into a potentially annihilating relationship with Jonathan is not exactly clear. Sandra had apparently been tricked, but Molly, at least originally, seeks out her fate and feels an affinity with him: "What is she doing? and why? she cannot shake the conviction that, when she speaks with James McEwan, when she is in James McEwan's presence, she is where she must be, where, in some mysterious sense, she belongs. Jonathan is too good for me—is that it? or is she too good for Jonathan?" (*LT,* 179). Indeed, the book raises questions about what is good: the studied repression of Jonathan or the more open hostility of James?

The point is that the fused relationship itself is bad: the twins have imperfectly divided human characteristics between themselves. Neither is a whole, and Molly is driven to know the whole, to release both herself and Jonathan from James's domination. Like the tortoiseshell cat made up of twin fetuses that "merge into a single organism within a few weeks" (*LT,* 81), James and Jonathan are in some ways locked into a single organism. James's need to dominate takes repulsive forms; brutal, sadistic, and vengeful, he is, Molly suspects, dangerous and unpredictable. He is associated throughout with destruction, with the death of love; he even sends Molly a heart that he claims is that of his pet cat.

While Sandra was destroyed through her relationship with James, Molly feels she must destroy James. Rather than turning her rage inward on herself in despair as Sandra did, she directs it toward James. At the end of the novel, she buys a gun and plans to free herself by killing her offender. He has invited her to his summer home on the beach, which he owns with Jonathan. But when Molly arrives, her belief that she can control the situation with a gun is quickly deflated; she learns that both twins are there, and she cannot distinguish who is who. Like an O. Henry story, the novel ends in suspension: "So Molly Marks stands on the windswept beach at Narragansett, in early April of a year she has scarcely registered, unmoving, transfixed, her right hand hidden in her shoulder bag, waiting. She looks from one of her lovers to the other. From one to the other" (*LT,* 236).

Molly Marks, like the reader, is unable to reconcile the perplexing dualities of human nature embodied in the McEwan twins and in her twinning with Sandra Shearer. Indeed, in assuming the pseudonym Rosamond Smith, Oates herself plays with the dualities of identity and of authorship. Perhaps she too is a divided self who feels a need to be released from her dominant identity as a well-known writer of long and complex novels in order to give play to another self, an unknown writer of slick psychological thrillers. Or perhaps the doubleness of Oates/Smith (which are indeed both legitimate surnames of the author) is deliberately part of the story—yet another manifestation of the omnipresent dualities dramatized in the novel.

What is interesting is that the dominant twin, Joyce Carol Oates, tried to hide the real identity of Rosamond Smith from the reader and from her publisher, but she was found out. Afterward, she promised publicly never to do such a thing again.[5] But she was at it again two years later, when the second novel of Rosamond Smith was published. Oates later claimed that she had promised never again to "attempt to write another secret pseudonymous novel—that is, secret from my agent and editor, as well as the rest of the world" (letter, 16 July 1990)—and that she has not done.

Soul/Mate

Soul/Mate (1989), which also plays on doubles, is another book written in the persona of Oates's pseudonymous double, Rosamond Smith. Only this time her own publisher, Dutton, brought out the book, with no reference to Oates but no real effort to conceal her identity either. The dust jacket reads, "Rosamond Smith lives in Princeton, New Jersey. She is now writing a new novel." The implication is certainly that Oates, having split her authorial self in two, is now comfortably proceeding to settle down and turn out novels by both "halves." Rosamond Smith is taking on an identity as a writer of slick psychological thrillers, and this one, with a blood-splattered heroine on the dust jacket, trails of gray blood on the chapter title pages, and black blood splotches between major sections, is insistently within this genre.

The book centers on a 28-year-old murderous psychopath, Colin Asch, and his fascination with a double, an alter ego—a beautiful, "pure" 39-year-old widow named Dorothea Deverell, whom he meets early in the novel when he appears, unexpected, at his aunt's dinner party. Dorothea is, he feels, his Shelley-like soul mate. Colin steeps himself in Shelley's poetry and acts out mad applications of Shelley's romanticism. This psychopathic personality becomes yet another portrait in Oates's stocked gallery of deluded romantics.

Like other of Oates's romantics, Colin Asch tries to shape reality to his will. His need to exert this control goes back, we learn through his aunt's gossip, to his tragic childhood. Both of his parents were killed when their automobile went off a bridge and submerged into the water. A 12-year-old child, he got out of the car and tried vainly to save them. The event is devastating: "it was said that Colin had gone mad in those minutes, that his mind simply shattered."[6] He feels the pull of death in that moment and his need to fight it: "I thought I could fight it, *controvert it!* . . . But the fact was I failed. The lesson I was meant to learn was—I failed. Life goes in one direction only, like a river flowing or like gravity—you can't controvert it" (*S/M*, 234–35).

He spent time in and out of hospitals and was, we gradually learn, apparently sexually and intellectually molested by the headmaster of his boarding school, who eventually committed suicide. "Will is the conduit of fate," Mr. Kreuzer had said, teaching Colin and a few other selected young boys that only one-tenth of one percent of human beings had the superior will to rule the world. Colin apparently feels himself to be one of those privileged few who can willfully control fate. In order to do so, his inner "evil twin" (*S/M*, 121) needs to be awakened and called into service.

A very attractive young man, Colin is charismatically charming to most women he encounters. A comment Oates made about another of her psychopathic charmers, Arnold Friend in "Where Are You Going, Where Have You Been?," applies equally well to Colin: "He charmed his victims as charismatic psychopaths have always charmed their victims, to the bewilderment of others who fancy themselves free of all lunatic attractions."[7] His appearance and charming manner belie his brutish, cruel evil twin. Party to his thoughts, the reader is likely to be shocked by his twisted, crude interior dialogue, his several murders and crimes, and his deranged epigrams, recorded in code in his secret blue ledger.

His instantaneous attraction to Dorothea, a well-respected, hardworking assistant director of a cultural institute, is reciprocated. She too feels an affinity with him, like a mother's for a son ("Had he lived to be born, my own son might be sitting in that place, Dorothea thought" [*S/M*, 22]). Later, after the dinner party, "Dorothea would recall how unmistakably, how seemingly naturally, their eyes had locked; how immediate her own reaction had been, of surprise, recognition, embarrassment" (*S/M*, 54).

Rather oddly, Dorothea concludes that Colin is "too like herself." She suspects that like herself, he has "a fatal lack of strength, drive, ambition. Not an excess but a deficiency of ego was the problem. . . . A tempestuous uncharted energy, like that of Shelley's West Wind, seemed to blow him about from place to place" (*S/M*, 66). While she is right that Colin is blown about by a "tempestuous uncharted energy," she—unlike her lover, Charles Carpenter, who grimly recognizes Colin for the psychopath he is—has no suspicions about the dark, evil propensities of this energy, which contrasts starkly with her own genuine "purity of conscience, or soul" (*S/M*, 128).

For Colin, Dorothea epitomizes the attraction of Shelley's "Soul Mate": "a soul out of his soul," a "heightened, externalised personality of himself, conceived as perfect; an ideal image of his own being; different in sex; his complement."[8] Like Shelley's soul mate in *Epipsychidion*, Dorothea, for

Colin, is at once a real woman, an archetype of feminine being, and the ideal of his own soul. Colin is like Shelley's Alastor, a young man vainly in search of the ideal. Dorothea seems to embody an otherworldly goodness and peace that shades into the lure of mystical egolessness, of idealized death itself, seen as a kind of all-embracing pantheism or nirvana. Colin records in his ledger, "Her influence is palpable as the moon's on the tide but it is an influence for peace, for calm, for love, for surrender. Not the fierce pounding surf but the gentle lapping on the beach like the approach of sleep. Like the joy of the Blue Room itself—no sound, no shadows! No gravity!" (*S/M*, 74). The Blue Room is a kind of suspension of consciousness in which "he [can] float for hours. For hours stretched like days, like an unbroken stream of fat clouds stretched across the sky. *And no one [can] touch him: he [is] bodiless, weightless, shadowless. Floating*" (*S/M*, 118).

Unfortunately for his victims, Colin doesn't remain in this disembodied state. In his adoration of Dorothea, in his need to be an instrument of fate, Colin, in the shape of his dark twin, "*performed to balance injustice, 'eye for an eye,' tooth for a tooth*" (*S/M*, 122). He feels he needs to right Dorothea's world, to make her happy. So, he kills her "enemy," Roger Krauss, an unsympathetic and critical board member at the institute, making possible Dorothea's selection as the director of the institute. Then he kills her lover's wife, making possible the long-delayed marriage of the lovers.

Dorothea's goodness, her "good kind decent generous soul," makes, he thinks, his action justified. He writes in his ledger: "ANYTHING DONE HENCEFORTH IS BLESSED BECAUSE IT EMANATES FROM THE SOUL" (*S/M*, 112). Paradoxically, Colin says, "*I want to be good! I want to destroy the world!*" (*S/M*, 197). He does indeed think that in his role as destroyer he is "paying *homage to the goodness in her*" (*S/M*, 199). He is like a "sleepwalker drawn to his fate. Not knowing what he would do but knowing, trusting; his instinct would guide him, for what did not, in this blessed state, emanate from the soul? In her presence *Colin Asch was elevated he was refined he was purified*" (*S/M*, 194).

Dorothea is puzzled, embarrassed, and troubled by Colin's unsolicited gifts and fawning adoration, although she does not suspect, until he kidnaps her, the degree of his madness. At an earlier point in their acquaintance, she had asked him directly what he wanted of her. He had replied, "*I don't want anything of you Dorothea only that you exist, that our lives are parallel.*" She thinks, shrewdly, that "parallel lines never meet." But Colin thinks of parallel lines meeting "at the horizon! Thus in the eye of the mind parallel lines NEVER FAIL to meet!" (*S/M*, 147). Dorothea is literally the other half of the world to him.

One day he shows up at Dorothea's house, tells her of the murders he has committed for her "as her agent," and takes her away to a deserted cabin in New Hampshire for "nearly one hundred hours of terror" (*S/M*, 224). He reveals to her more of his derangement by claiming that his murders are simply his way of attempting to set the world in order: "You know what Shelley said of himself: 'I go my way like a sleepwalker. . . . I go until I am stopped and I never *am* stopped'" (*S/M*, 219). Yet, increasingly petulant, he is "not *happy* the way I deserve . . . I need your *help*, Dorothea—your *advice* and *consolation*! . . . I need some sign from you that things are all right. That, you know things are—in place again" (*S/M*, 222).

Finally, he tries to get Dorothea to agree willingly to participate in a death ceremony, pressing a knife into her fingers just as his schoolmaster had apparently forced one into his years before, when he had attempted a similar double death. Dorothea struggles free; the knife falls to the floor. Colin picks it up, holding it against his own throat, saying reproachfully: "Don't you want to? Don't you love me? You'll let me do it alone?" (*S/M*, 239). She stares at him calmly "as if he were staring into a mirror at his own reflection," as indeed he is, in the sense that she is his own narcissistic projection of his soul mate. Then, with "unspeakable pleasure," he slashes his own throat; blood explodes onto Dorothea, marking her "for life."

The epilogue details the marriage and house plans of Dorothea and Charles Carpenter, whose romance works out, after all, rather conveniently —although neither is in the least implicated in Colin's madness. Dorothea thinks of Colin as standing "on the far side of an abyss . . . speaking to me, trying to explain himself, in a normal voice—but a normal voice, under the circumstances, isn't sufficient. *I can't hear*" (*S/M*, 247). "Let it go," says Charles, and wisely, she does.

Dorothea can let go of her dark double; can Joyce Carol Oates? Apparently not—or not yet, anyway. She has recently published yet another novel, *Nemesis* (1990), under this pseudonym and admits, "I have plans for one beyond that, but, perhaps, no more!" (letter, 16 July 1990).

Nemesis

Nemesis, with strong thematic affinities with Oates's other two pseudonymous novels, is the strongest of Rosamond Smith's thriller mysteries. It gains resonance and authenticity by being set in the academic world Oates knows so well. Indeed, its added piquancy is that it is a fictionalized takeoff of a well-publicized scandal at Princeton regarding the alleged rape of a male student by an esteemed English professor, the handling of which provoked a great deal of commentary and criticism in the Princeton community.[9]

The setting of *Nemesis* is Forest Park Conservatory of Music in Connecticut. Early in the novel, after a party at the home of Maggie Blackburn, a pianist who is also director of the Music Education Program for Advanced Students, Rolfe Christensen, a distinguished composer in residence, rapes a young graduate student, Brendan Bauer. Later Christensen is murdered by eating a poisoned chocolate from a gift box anonymously sent to him. Shortly thereafter the mysteries proliferate when his executor, Nicholas Reickmann, is also brutally slain. Brendan Bauer is accused of the murders, and his teacher, Maggie Blackburn, becomes his defender. Cutting her long and beautiful hair and taking on the investigative acumen of her now-deceased father, she becomes Nemesis, the goddess of retribution. In the surprising turns of plot, she "brings down immoderate good fortune and the presumption that attends it and is the punisher of extraordinary crimes" (from the definition of *Nemesis* in the *Oxford English Dictionary*).

Maggie is a type of woman Oates/Smith has portrayed before, most recently in Dorothea Deverell, the beautiful, "pure," but rather pliant heroine of *Soul/Mate*. Maggie is "a transparency to herself but something of an enigma to others."[10] She is unmarried, self-effacing, removed, beautiful, but somewhat sexless. In fact, one of her suitors breaks off this relationship with this dismissal: "In my opinion, Maggie, you're hardly a woman at all" (*N*, 13).

Indeed, this novel's plot twists amid the ambiguities of gender identity, often turning upside down the prototypical male and female roles. The rape of Brendan Bauer, a young, straight male student, turns him into a "womanly" victim who goes to his female teacher for protection and assistance. In fact, from the first, the affinities between Brendan and Maggie are stressed: "She saw in him, in his eager yet retreating attitude, in his somber, plain, intense face, even in the slope of his thin shoulders, something of herself: he might have been a younger brother of hers, a distant cousin" (*N*, 19). Brendan is, in effect, Maggie's soul mate, her male twin or brother or cousin, to whom she feels a special bond. His victimization is in a sense hers; that Brendan met Christensen at her house seems to implicate her in the crime and its consequences.

Yet Maggie harbors, like Dorothea in *Soul/Mate*, a secret passion for a strong-willed, overtly masculine married man, Calvin Gould, the provost of the conservatory. Not only is Maggie romantically attracted to him, but she also holds him in high esteem: "She would hear no ill of the man. *Could* hear no ill. If forced to she turned very pale, or blushed fiercely, or leapt to defend him, often indiscreetly" (*N*, 24). Perhaps because there is also a strong married man to whom the heroine is attracted in *Soul/Mate,* our expectation is that somehow this relationship will work out.

But Calvin Gould's handling of the rape is not all that it could be. Although he is initially shocked and sympathetic when Maggie reports the incident to him, he eventually arranges what is essentially a cover-up. Bauer agrees not to press criminal charges, and Christensen is suspended from teaching but retains "his office on campus, his rights and privileges as a faculty member, his rank as Distinguished Professor and Composer-in-Residence," and his "enormous salary" (*N,* 84–85). Later, after Christensen's murder, Maggie and Gould's relationship is intensified by their deep engagement in the events and their incipient erotic attraction. Gould tries to dissuade Maggie from her steadfast presumption of Brendan's innocence. Maggie, lulled by her intense feelings for Gould, fails to register the significance of some observations, such as her recognition that Gould and his wife Naomi resemble one another; in fact, "*[aren't] their profiles identical?*" (*N,* 151).

Eventually, though, Maggie must abandon her romantic vision and put on the methods of her father, who had been a trial lawyer, an assistant district attorney, and a judge: "*Suspect everyone. It is guilt that should be assumed, not innocence*" (*N,* 203). Cutting her hair, she also shuns male assistance, whether that of Gould or of the police detective assigned to the case.

Through her investigations she discovers a previous connection between Christensen and Gould, and Gould's misrepresentation of details of that past. She also discovers the surprising fact that Gould and his supposed wife Naomi are twins. Just when Maggie is puzzling through all these pieces with dread, Gould shows up at her house. In a wonderfully suspenseful scene, filled with romantic attraction and cold-blooded fear, is revealed gradually to Maggie's consciousness (and to the reader) the face of the murderer, superimposed on the desired lover: "He had kissed her, hadn't he?— but his lips were cold, hard, without love, a kind of interrogation, and his fingers framing her face had been viselike, tight enough to cause discomfort. *How many times you'd dreamt of that man kissing you—and so he has! Poor fool!*" (*N,* 237).

When Gould shows up at her house for a second time in the same evening, the game is up: he knows that Maggie knows his role in the murders. He reveals to her his own dark past, the fact that he was, at age 17, seduced by Christensen, victimized, desexed: "And afterward, Christensen had this strange power over me . . . the power of forcing a victim into complicity. That was the true shame of it. *It was as if he'd turned me into a woman*" (*N,* 244).

His manhood compromised in some fundamental way, he cannot sustain

his marriage to a beautiful and unfaithful wife, Naomi. And, further com-
pounding his identity problems, he is a twin tied inextricably to his sister
Caroline: "it's as if we are a single person, a single organism sharing a nervous
system, memory, instincts . . . but nothing else. . . . I hate the connection between us, I've always hated it . . . but there it is. I couldn't escape her if I
wanted to, and she couldn't escape me" (N, 255–56). His sister, mentally in-
jured in a childhood accident, lives with him and is presumed to be his wife;
their twinning bond remains intact. Adding to the book's reversal of prototypical gender roles, she is the dark shadow who becomes his avenger. Apparently sensing Christensen's role in Brendan's rape and his violation of her
brother in the past, Caroline sends the poisoned chocolates to Christensen, although here too her brother tries to protect her by insisting to Maggie that he
committed this murder. He does commit the second one; when Reickmann
unravels some of the mystery, Gould kills him, just as he intends to destroy
Maggie because of her discoveries. But although he attacks Maggie, he does
not kill her; she is discovered unconscious the next morning by Brendan.
Gould himself dies that night by running his car off the road.

Maggie, later reflecting on the events, realizes that Gould had decided
not to kill her "to choose me over her. *Her* waiting for him in their house"
(N, 268). His sister Caroline, after his death, becomes totally incapacitated
and permanently hospitalized, "so Calvin had punished both himself and
his twin, Maggie thought" (N, 269). Tortured, conflicted, fundamentally
incomplete, with his identity hopelessly bifurcated, his manhood tragically
violated, Gould evokes, finally, some sympathy. And Maggie retains some
of her romantic attraction to him: she attempts to suppress "her deep un-
happiness and dismay at having lost the man irrevocably . . . even as she
knew such a sentiment was grotesque" (N, 272).

In fact, the only truly unregenerate and unsympathetic person in the
book is Christensen. His messes and his victims are vividly detailed from
the opening scenes at Maggie's party: the damp towel he leaves behind in
Maggie's bathroom, "twisted from the rack as if its neck had been wrung";
the toilet seat "splashed with his pungent urine"; the room contaminated by
the "acrid odor" of his cigar smoke; the dead canary killed by the cold blast
of air from the window he had carelessly opened. These are of course merely
preludes to the excruciatingly vivid portrayal of his rape of Brendan—just
one in a series, we learn, of such brutish encounters.

Brendan, despite his misfortune and trials, survives through the interven-
tion of his avenging "twin," Maggie. In the epilogue we learn that Maggie
and Brendan, she a professor and he a graduate student, have moved to
Minneapolis, where they live together companionably and happily. Their

status is undefined and a matter of speculation to their friends and acquaintances; Brendan could be "living *in* her house but not living *with* her. Then again, they often displayed affection for each other, of a kind. So perhaps in fact they were lovers" (*N*, 274). To casual acquaintances it looks, because of the "similarity between them—height, body type, skin tone, manner—that the two might be sister and brother" (*N*, 275). The implication is that they live a kind of androgynous duality, each having developed both the male and the female sides of being. Their harmony is emblematized, in the final scene, in the pair of canaries Brendan gives to Maggie to replace the ones she had lost earlier.

So *Nemesis*, like *Lives of Twins* and *Soul/Mate*, is another thriller mystery, another exploration of the rich potentialities of the theme of twinning, of the problematics of self and other that so obsess Joyce Carol Oates. Has Oates herself discovered a twin, an other, in Rosamond Smith—one who justifies her separate existence? In her essay "Pseudonymous Selves," she says that "in the end, it is probable that the cultivation of a pseudonym is not so very different from the cultivation *in vivo* of the narrative voice that sustains any work of words, making it unique and inimitable. Choosing a pseudonym as the work's formal author simply takes the mysterious process a step or two further, erasing the author's social identity and supplanting it with a pseudonymous identity" ("Pseudonymous," 396–97). But since the secret is out—since we know that Smith and Oates are one and the same, are in fact soul mates—it is unclear what exactly is gained from this disguise. Perhaps what is gained is simply the freedom to be a genre writer, a producer of mystery novels, or what Oates has called concept novels: "A real novel is many-layered, complex, with lots of different characters and subplots, but the language is terribly important. But a concept novel is more like a movie scenario, with lots of dialogue."[11]

Oates's publishing as her pseudonymous self is a playful attempt to get out from under the scrutinizing, judging, pigeonholing judgments of critics: "For who among us, identified with such confidence by others, had not felt uneasy, if not an impostor, knowing that, whatever they know of us, *we* do not somehow share that knowledge? Fame's carapace does not allow for easy breathing" ("Pseudonymous," 397). Judge these works differently, Oates/Smith seems to say: use different standards. I suppose one should, but the temptation is strong to read these works simply as further examples of the variegated skill of Joyce Carol Oates.

Chapter Six
Appetites and Bitter Hearts

While dissimilar in many ways, *American Appetites* (1989) and *Because It Is Bitter, and Because It Is My Heart* (1990) are alike in the critical perspectives both offer on the American dream—the aspiration for "the good life" fundamental to American culture. They approach the subject from quite different angles, however. One book is about a middle-aged couple who seem to be living embodiments of a fulfilled dream: affluent, privileged, successful, upper-middle-class professionals. The other is about two adolescents, one white, one black, growing up in a seedy, bleak, lower-middle-class world in a small city in upper New York State; theirs is a dream yet to be achieved. Yet early in both novels, the characters' worlds are fractured by an unintentional killing. In *American Appetites* the husband pushes his wife through the plate-glass window of their dining room during an argument, and she later dies. In *Because It Is Bitter, and Because It Is My Heart* the black youth, while escorting the white girl home, kills a white boy in self-defense. Violence in both novels, as in so many other of Oates's works, is the result of tensions, longings, and frustrations that break through the civil games of society, the outward trappings of character.

American Appetites

American Appetites records the crack-up of the prototypical American success story, and it offers very little hope for fulfillment of the inchoate American appetites that contribute to its demise. The novel is about a middle-aged couple, Ian and Glynnis McCullough, who live in a beautiful house in a beautiful neighborhood, surrounded by convivial friends. Theirs is "a life complex beyond his reckoning: a normal life, the life of the species, yet uniquely American. Marriage, children, a job, a position, property acquired and protected, and, in time, a place in a community: a reputation."[1] Ian is a senior fellow at the prestigious Institute for Independent Research in the Social Sciences. His work involves seeing the individual as part of a socially predictable unit: "compiling, charting, graphing, predicting. Calibrating the diverse ways in which, so seemingly individual, the individual becomes a mathematical unit of a certain coherence—in a certain system, at least," even though he had always "thought it rather terrifying that unrelated individuals, wholly unaware of one another, nonetheless cooperated in a collective destiny" (*AA*, 6). The acting out of a collective destiny, a life of the species, a uniquely American life, is exactly what the story of the McCulloughs is about. (Oates claims that "the novel is very Princeton— could not have been written elsewhere" [letter, 16 July 1990].)

The central climactic incident of the book occurs at home one evening, when Glynnis confronts Ian about what she believes is his infidelity with a young acquaintance of hers, Sigrid Hunt. She had discovered the cancelled check for $1,000 that Ian had given to the young woman. Drunk, accusatory, and increasingly out of control, Glynnis verbally and then physically attacks her husband, wielding a steak knife. He shoves her away from him, and she falls through a plate-glass window. After being in a coma for 18 days, she dies. Shortly thereafter, Ian is accused of murder. The novel records Ian's bemused state through the stages of the legal process: the indictment, trial, and eventual acquittal. He is saved by the eleventh-hour appearance of Sigrid Hunt, who had been in hiding. She testifies that he had befriended her in a time of need and that he had not had an affair with her.

Sigrid's appearance and testimony stir in Ian some new hope and a wish to save himself. He agrees finally to testify in his own behalf and makes a very credible defense of himself, "for he was, after all, the most civilized of men." He explains that while he is not guilty of murder, he is guilty of killing his wife because he acted blindly, "in an animal panic," pushing her away from him, not knowing what the consequences would be. He claims that it seemed as if the "fabric of our lives . . . had been turned inside out . . . exposed in reverse, like a photograph negative." His wife had seemed a total stranger to him; his response had been that of a stranger. He hadn't wanted to tell anyone, "because it was a violation of my wife's honor, and a violation of our marriage. I didn't want to seem to have made her into an adversary when in a very real way she had not been, had never been. It was only this madness that came upon us . . . this sudden terrible fury that has ruined our lives" (*AA*, 318–19).

While Ian's testimony makes a "profound impression" on the judge and jury and secures his legal acquittal, the life he had built with Glynnis is shattered. The novel is about the brittle fragility of the structures and institutions that shape the typical American life-style. It is also about the other side of the looking glass, the "photograph negative," the dark other in the self and in others, which Ian encounters as a result of this experience. The novel is ruthlessly honest in its assessment of both the satisfactions and dissatisfactions of living out the American dream.

At the outset of the novel, Ian and Glynnis have in many respects an orderly and fulfilling life. They exemplify the best of civilized virtues. Later, at the trial, others attest that "Dr. Ian McCullough was now a man of 'unfailing courtesy,' 'kindness,' 'generosity': a model husband and father, a model citizen, a model of professional 'brilliance' and 'reliability'; admired by his colleagues, loved by his friends; 'even-tempered,' 'rational,' 'reasonable': even, in the passionate words of an Institute colleague (Denis Grinnel), 'the most civilized man of my acquaintance'" (AA, 300). Glynnis, admired by her friends, an exceptional hostess and cook who writes popular cookbooks, is at work on a cookbook entitled American Appetites when the novel opens.

Indeed, appetites—hungers, ambitions, inchoate longings—are forces that contribute to a vague restlessness in the McCulloughs and their friends. They have achieved the American dream and don't know what to do now. "My success is my problem" says Ian, "and his friends laughed with him and agreed, for many of them were burdened with the same problem: they were, like Ian McCullough, successes 'in their fields,' well into middle age yet 'still youthful,' comfortably well off beyond all dreams and expectations of graduate-student days yet still 'ambitious'—though ambitious for what, none could have said" (AA, 7). Glynnis feels that all their friends and associates are in fact "hungry; that ambition was in fact hunger: very nearly visceral, physiological, 'real.' And since hunger is nature, it is surely natural; isn't it?" (AA, 7).

At times Glynnis gets great pleasure and satisfaction in contemplating their achieved success: "Glynnis thinks in triumph, My house. My family. My life. Mine" (AA, 68). At other times, however, she is aware of their life's utter fragility: "Our house is made of glass, Glynnis thought, and our lives are made of glass; and there is nothing we can do to protect ourselves" (AA, 55). In a world that values youth and appearance, aging is especially difficult: "They say of course that it is the body that betrays; the self, the soul, remains inviolate; thus you are twenty years old so abruptly, so rudely, in a fifty-year-old body. And your journey has only now begun. I cannot bear it, Glynnis thinks. Something will happen and it will happen soon and it will happen without my volition or responsibility: but what?" (AA, 65).

The book opens with "Prologue: The Creation of the World," in which Ian and Glynnis are depicted as "young lovers, and married; and hand in hand," seeing Europe together. Growing out of young love is the world they create together, and now they are bonded, twins: "for he seems to inhabit her, like an indwelling spirit that is both other and herself: a twin" (AA, 39).

But much remains that is private, unknown, and mysterious; over time, they bear the scars of the many failures and emotional vicissitudes of their marriage. In the quarrel that precipitates the accident, Ian learns, to his surprise, about Glynnis's infidelities, her "self hatred." In attempting to assess his role in the accident, he thinks that he had both "intended it; and . . . not intended it (and this *was* the paradox but he'd known what he did" (*AA*, 130). The violence that erupts in their world, as is so often the case in Oates's fictional universe, is an expression of tensions forcing their way up to the surface of life from deep in the psyche—tensions denied in the surface structures of their Hazelton life. These encounters with the unknown, the unexpected, these eruptions of violence, are the gothic dark side of personal and societal relationships.

The novel poignantly shows that the lives people lead, the roles they assume, the structures they build around themselves cannot minister to an inner emptiness, a visceral and undefined hunger. Ian, in fact, is preoccupied with a search for the soul: he is overcome by "a certitude that we are all in disguise from one another and from ourselves, souls glimmering like phosphorescent fire, hidden in the opacity of flesh" (*AA*, 100). Underneath the surface of propriety and respectability, success and happiness, are often baser emotions, unmet needs, American appetites, unfulfilled souls.

While Ian does not literally have an affair with Sigrid Hunt, he does allow himself to drift into a compromising, clandestine relationship with her; he does think about her a great deal and is unable to resist the tempting lure away from his orderly, structured world. During the ordeal of his indictment and trial, he seems totally disconnected from his successful self, his public image; his friends comment that he does not seem to remember "who he is." In line with the looking-glass motif, he seems to have drifted into a surreal wonderland separated from the familiar by a pane of glass: "Other people are real enough, other people . . . but on the other side of a sort of barrier from me: a gigantic pane of glass. This time I don't want to break the glass" (*AA*, 243). Rather than wanting to connect with his previous self, he exists in a dreamlike state. He gets involved in a sordid liaison with Meika Cassity, the wife of one of his friends; he is alternately attracted and repelled by her, alternately indifferent and groveling. Meanwhile, the trial goes on, essentially in another realm: it seems a kind of game in which Ian is only vaguely interested.

The suburban life the McCulloughs have been living is another game. What appear to be solid, respectable lives and faithful, happy marriages are only the civil trappings of a much different reality full of rage, infidelity, and desperation. Frustrated by his broken marriage to Roberta, Denis exclaims to Ian: "the women of Hazleton, the wives, playing an elaborate game . . . behind our backs. We are the game, but we can't see it. The way they simulate happiness, answering the telephone, opening the door to guests, where, a moment before, there was something very different . . . from happiness" (AA, 235).

Before Sigrid's reappearance, Ian had been volitionlessly drifting toward death; now, "in a transport of wonder," he thinks, "I want to live." He experiences a kind of instantaneous attraction to Sigrid and a belief in the potentialities of a relationship with her: "That she loved him or might love him, that his life had not after all ended, that he was not condemned to a posthumous existence after all . . . but a life like the old life, even more wonderful than the old, for its impurities had been blasted away: this seemed to him the miraculous, the unspeakably miraculous thing. And it was within his grasp, was it not?" (AA, 317). Ian, an awakened romantic, believes he can transcend all this hardship, move beyond his old life, and create with Sigrid a new world.

In the epilogue, paralleling ironically the prologue, Ian and Sigrid do indeed establish a new life together; vacationing in Maine, they entertain two of his old friends. We learn that on the very night of the verdict they had become lovers. Theirs seems the perfect realization of a destined love: "In a delirium of happiness in Sigrid Hunt's rather strong arms, Ian McCullough thought, I have loved her all along; I have always loved her" (AA, 331). This would seem to be a fantasy-come-true ending: Ian able to start his life all over again with a young and beautiful woman, who is in fact hauntingly reminiscent, with her red hair, of the young Glynnis. But a chilling bit of Ian's stream-of-consciousness is interjected into the narrative. Thinking how much he loves his friends, he realizes he will never see them again. And "how do you know?", he asks himself:

> I just know.
> Yes, but how?
> I will blow my brains out when the season turns. (AA, 337)

Despite the convivial front he maintains, Ian's despair is deep. He thinks now of his father in his final few months, before he had blown his brains out: "His brain had been muddled by alcohol and, Ian now saw, so very simply, despair" (AA, 339).

This grim conclusion posits no alternative, no hope. Ian can find no reason to live. He cannot repeat the past, and now older and wiser, he does not want to—even though Sigrid, an image of the young Glynnis, seems to offer that possibility. The vagaries of sexual union will not sustain him. His work no longer compels. The social structures he has built are fractured and unsustaining.

This is a devastating portrait because Ian is such a fine example of the civilized, successful, upper-middle-class American. In reaching the empty heart of darkness at the core of the American dream—the depletion of idealism, the pointlessness of personal ambition and aspiration—he can be seen to be acting out a collective fate. What is left are the inchoate hungers, longings, appetites of the soul.

All Oates's books are reflections on the tensions and conflicts within our culture, and this novel is in particular. It is a kind of summing up of what might be called the death throes of the American dream. Moreover, it is unrelieved in its negativism, bringing in no alternate contexts, suggesting no other possibilities, although certainly the reader may feel compelled to posit some: what of the natural world, of other cultures, of social issues, of political concerns? The American dream, as pursued by Ian and his upper-middle-class friends, is a little island of self-absorption separated from all else. It is a cultural narcissism that ultimately collapses onto itself.

I should note, though, that Oates cautions against an "entirely negative" reading of the novel, pointing out the transformation of Ian's daughter, who is "turned from a spoiled adolescent into an idealistic young woman. (In my eyes utterly 'real'—I know the power of shock to transform us)". She also notes that Ian only contemplates suicide: "'contemplation' of suicide is very common; he may or he may not" (letter, 16 July 1990).

Because It Is Bitter, and Because It Is My Heart

Because It Is Bitter, and Because It Is My Heart (1990) is one of Oates's finest novels, in part because it is so deftly written. In memorable and luminous prose, Oates evokes her quintessential themes: the palpable reality of the bleak, seedy industrial town (in this case, Hammond in upper New York State) and the experiences of adolescence. Racial tensions infuse the story, adding a rich new dimension to Oates's examination of American character and experience. In boldly delving into the consciousnesses of black as well as white characters, Oates renders "the lineaments of racial resentment with precision," according to Henry Louis Gates, who finds "her ear [to be] unfailing across gradations of class and color."[2] The novel is, I think, a necessary counterpoint to *American Appetites*. The enclosed, privileged, professional, upper-middle-class world of the earlier novel begs for a balance, a wider canvas that takes in the underclass, white and black, of our complex, interracial American society.

Iris Courtney, a white 14-year-old, is taunted and threatened one evening by a malicious, vicious, deranged young white man, Red Garlock, while attempting to return to her lower-middle-class neighborhood after a foray into the "wrong" side of town. She enters a store where a black fellow high-school student and basketball star, Jinx Fairchild, works. He volunteers to walk Iris home. A fight between the two young men ensues, during which Jinx kills Red in self-defense. Because Jinx is black, Red is white, and the year is 1956, the characters know that this act is not likely to meet with color-blind justice. Jinx urges Iris to go home. He then dumps Red's body in the river, thus beginning a lifetime of cover-up and complicity between himself and Iris. Their role in the incident is never discovered; sustained throughout the novel, for the bonded characters and the reader alike, is the tension of that secret.

Convinced that she is responsible and that Jinx is guiltless, Iris adroitly misleads the police by suggesting that a white motorcycle gang had been involved in Red's death. She is obsessed with the "blood bondage" that locks Jinx and herself in a special relationship. She seeks out opportunities to cross Jinx's path, to communicate with him: "*No one is so close to me as you. No one is so close to us as we are to each other.*"[3] Jinx's state of mind is vividly rendered: he is baffled by Iris's attentions and profoundly shaken by the experience. He has a great desire to confess, to atone; he waits for God to punish him. He is unable to put the matter out of his mind. Finally, in an act that Iris recognizes as self-inflicted punishment for his crime, he cracks his ankle coming down from a jump shot at a basketball game, destroying forever his chances of pursuing his aspirations through that sport.

The novel parallels and counterpoints the subsequent lives of these two children from inauspicious backgrounds—their ambitions, their spiritual longings, their preoccupation with this experience, and especially their inchoate connection. Oates uses their "blood bondage" as an emblem of the visceral curiosity, awareness, attraction, antagonism, fear, and electricity between the races, which simmer under the surface of the biracial society in America before the civil rights movement.

While the novel does move in time through the beginnings of the sixties, the Fairchilds do not participate in civil rights activism. Jinx's mother, who works most of her life for a white physician, tries to raise her children with middle-class values and aspirations. Her oldest son, Sugar Baby, whose head is turned by the glitz and glamour of underworld crime, ultimately meets a violent end, but she has high hopes for Jinx, a good student and good athlete. After the basketball accident, she is bitterly disappointed when he refuses to conform to "white folks' expectations," rejects all "*performing monkey*" routines (BB, 239, 195).

On the PBS program "Bookmark" in April 1990, Oates acknowledged that the book is informed by both her own high-school passion for basketball (she was on the girls' "honor team" and drew on her own experience for the basketball scenes) and her strong interest in the role of the black athlete in America. She is aware of the incredible pressures to perform brought to bear on the outstanding black athlete. Jinx, ruined by the incident with Red, opts out of this pressure and chooses instead to lead the life of a "typical" unaspiring black man. He drops out of school in his senior year, gets married, begets children, and works for the sanitation department. Yet he is restlessly unfulfilled, subject to desperate longings, plagued by a sense of inauthenticity, emptiness, coldness. His basketball nickname, "Iceman," meant to describe his cool savvy, also is a commentary on his deadened emotions. And in this, as in many other aspects of his life, he has a soul mate in Iris, who is also cold-hearted, isolated, unfulfilled. (Oates takes the title of the novel from Stephen Crane's poem "The Black Riders," in which a "naked, bestial" creature eats his heart in a desert. Asked if it is good, the creature replies, "I like it / Because it is bitter, / And because it is my heart."[4]

Iris has more options than Jinx, not only because of her color but also because of her shrewd intelligence, duplicity, and opportunism. While Jinx is jinxed, subject to bad luck, Iris, named for the eye, is clear-sighted, able to move beyond obstacles and limitations. As in so many of Oates's novels, the mother is a powerful presence in the daughter's life. Iris's mother, Persia, is a strikingly beautiful woman who tries desperately to hang on to vestiges of seedy glamour as she ages and who ultimately drinks herself into fatal illness. Iris's father, on a downward career trajectory in sales, management, public relations, and gambling enterprises, is a shadowy presence, absent for long periods during Iris's adolescence.

Paralleling characters in many of Oates's other stories, including Marya, and Enid in *You Must Remember This,* Iris is bookish and successful in school. Her scholarship to Syracuse University is a ticket out of her impoverished rearing. She becomes the assistant to Professor Savage, who along with his wife befriends her. She opportunistically latches on to them, even though she is cynically clear-sighted about their blindness to their own extraordinary privilege: "Iris perceives too that her friends' [the Savages'] very magnanimity is granted them by means of an infrastructure that surrounds and protects them yet remains unexamined as the air they breathe: their inherited wealth, their social position, the color of their skin. The Savages' great good fortune is an accident of history they seem to assume is not accidental but natural . . . their God-given birthright" (BB, 312). Their name is ironic; they are exemplars of the most civilized of human traits, and any savagery is suppressed or denied. Iris also denies any unsavoriness in her past: she rewrites it for the Savages, mythologizing her mother into a saintly figure and recasting her father, giving him the mystery, idealism, and sense of respectability he lacks. When she meets the Savages' son of marriageable age, she thinks calmly, "You're the one" (BB, 324), and by the end of the novel their marriage is about to transpire.

But before this happens, Iris too—in parallel with her dark double, Jinx—seems to be seeking out punishment and atonement in an unarticulated way. She too is longing for meaning, for goodness, for a sense of authentic identity. The one "real" experience in her life continues to be the "blood bondage" she has with Jinx. On the day of the assassination of President Kennedy (which occurs while she is a student at Syracuse University), she wanders into a black neighborhood, where she is eventually picked up and beaten by a gang of black youths.

It is hard to know precisely how to interpret Iris's motivation in going to the black neighborhood on that day. The incident certainly parallels the one with Red Garlock, only this time blacks—surrogates for Jinx, perhaps— beat her up. She appears to be seeking connection to the black "other" world of American society and especially to her black double, Jinx, to whom she is so attracted and about whom she feels so guilty. She tells him several times, "I am the one. You were never to blame. I am the one" (BB, 161). She has always been fascinated by blacks, who seem to her to have more "reality" than whites: "glancing down at her white skin, she feels a sense of vertigo, a physical sickness, as if its whiteness were the outward symptom of her spirit's etiolation, a profound and unspeakable not-thereness" (BB, 155). She says once as a young girl: "If I was colored . . . I'd know who I was" (BB, 93). In commenting on the book, Oates claims that Iris needs to "exorcise" her overwhelming "attraction to, yearning for black people." Racial discrimination, says the author, is a "mutual loss," and the "gravitational pull" between the races is experienced deeply by Iris.[5]

Jinx for the most part rebuffs Iris's several overtures to him. Only once do they have a moment of intimacy; it happens after he drops out of high school and gets married. She asks him to meet her at a restaurant. They go for a drive together, which ends with Jinx tenderly holding, fondling, and comforting her as she tries to explain what she wants from him: "I don't want anything from you but the fact of you. I don't even love you, really . . . it isn't that. I know you're married, and . . . it isn't that really, it's just that there's no one but you, for me. And there *isn't* you . . . I know that. Please don't misunderstand me, I know that" (*BB*, 242). Aware of the visceral attraction in their relationship, its potential for sexuality and for violence, he is pleased that he can keep himself in check and give her all she wants from him, sensing "her aloneness that's keener and more painful than his own . . . mixed up with her sad white skin. The legendary aloneness and cold-heartedness of white folks" (*BB*, 244).

Yet they are more alike than Jinx recognizes or acknowledges. He, like Iris, is unable to feel authentic, connected. He leads a life of quiet desperation. Finally, he is unable to resist the lure of the military, of the signs proclaiming "Uncle Sam Wants You." Near the end of the novel he enlists, an action laden with irony. He who had sought to avoid "white folks' expectations" is drawn to the most tragic stereotype, that of the GI in the futile Vietnam War—a conflict fueled disproportionately by black blood. But perhaps Jinx realizes that this too is a prescribed part that he can use for his own ends. Indeed, his own ironic perspective and continuing feeling of disconnection are evident in the note he leaves on the back of a picture of himself for Iris: "*Honey—Think I'll 'pass'?*" (*BB*, 403)—a question that evokes Iris's most intense grief over the loss of her potent but unfulfilled connection to another.

In the epilogue, as Iris tries on her wedding gown for the last time, she too questions her ability to play the role she has chosen for herself. She asks, "Do you think I look the part?" Apparently she does; she "passes" quite well. But there is a flash-forward indicating that her continuing coldness baffles and upsets her husband: "icy-hearted, harder than nails, her husband will one day say in hurt in outrage in simple bewilderment, Why did you marry me if, why do you insist you love me if" (*BB*, 377). This novel is, as the author herself explains, "a tragedy in the guise of romance" ("Bookmark"). Although it has a conventional ending—a marriage that is also an act of social betterment for the heroine—it is a tragedy of estrangement, of loss.

In fact, this book may seem even grimmer than *American Appetites* because its disillusioned characters are so young. While Ian McCullough of the latter novel reaches the dead end of the American dream and intends to blow his brains out, Iris and Jinx have no choice but to try to "pass," to try to "look the part." They are too young to be so cynical, but they are also too young to quit. They have tasted the bitter, empty heart of aspiration before achieving its fruits. Yet perhaps I overstate the case. Both are survivors. Both shape themselves energetically, deliberately, out of choices they make; both play the game, even though they know it is just a game. Oates's explanation of the "psychological implications" of *Alice in Wonderland and*

Through the Looking Glass seems particularly relevant to similar aspects of her own work, and to her most recent books in particular: "Though one can be detached from the activities of life, seeing them as no more than games, it is necessary to get down there in the game as well, to play it with as much enthusiasm as possible. Everyone is playing and no one is left out. The game is *being played* and we are all participants, not really controlling the game, but fulfilling it in some existential, mysterious way. In any case, a victory of some kind is assured."[6]

The "victory" here is uncertain, but I believe it lies in the very aspirations of Oates's characters and in their failure to be satisfied. In their restless desire for more than empty game-playing, in their longing for authenticity and connection, lies hope for them personally and for our culture. Oates has said: "in my fiction, the troubled people are precisely those who yearn for a higher life—those in whom the life-form itself is stirring" (Boesky, 482). This particular novel, she says, is about the "auto-genetic creation of self," the need to invent the self as one goes along ("Bookmark").

All of Oates's work demonstrates the central importance of authentic individuality to American civilization and American culture—and the difficulty of achieving it. Individuals need to get beyond the enclosing paranoid delusions of our culture, beyond rigid categorizations and stratifications. In *American Appetites,* Ian's choice finally not to "play the game" is merely his personal defeat, not necessarily a cultural defeat. In contrast, in *Because It Is Bitter,* Iris and Jinx choose to play, to use their wits to survive (unless, of course, one sees Jinx's choice of the soldierly role as a quest for death). And although bonded, they imperfectly understand the significance of their connection. Theirs is reminiscent of other bonded sibling relationships in Oates's fiction, such as those between Jules and Maureen in *them,* Laney and Vale in *Childwold,* and Kirsten and Owen in *Angel of Light.* Although not siblings, they are locked in "blood bondage"; their connection emblematizes the psychological and sociological dualities of our culture and the inchoate longing for oneness, for unity with the other, at the heart of the American dream.

Chapter Seven
Critical Contexts and Contradictions

Through over 25 years of sustained productivity, Joyce Carol Oates has created an impressive and variegated body of work. "She certainly tried" is the epitaph she wryly suggests for her tombstone.[1] She is a writer seriously and obsessively dedicated to her craft; it is, she says simply, her "life's commitment." Her name is well known in literate circles in the United States and Europe. At a reception at the Soviet Embassy in December 1987, Raisa Gorbachev singled her out as an American writer "much read" and "much admired" by Soviets, including the first lady herself.[2] Oates has for several years been shortlisted for the Nobel Prize. She was elected a member of the American Academy and Institute of Arts and Letters in 1978. In 1970 she received the National Book Award for her novel *them,* and she is the recipient of several other awards from the Guggenheim Foundation, the National Institute of Arts and Letters, and the Lotus Club, among others; she is also a three-time winner of the Continuing Achievement Award in the O. Henry Prize Stories series.

Yet in spite of this public and professional recognition, and in spite of her literal and figurative residence in academia, Oates's corpus was for many years treated with indifference by much of the academic community. To be sure, this is changing. She is the subject of a growing number of dissertations and books. Her archive is now housed at Syracuse University. Recently taken up by feminist critics and studied in modern literature couses on many campuses, she has also been invited to many universities in the last few years, including Stanford, Yale, Duke, Wisconsin, Louisiana State, Skidmore, New York University, Columbia, Michigan, the University of California at Los Angeles, Texas, North Carolina, Virginia, Iowa, Oregon, Washington, and Wesleyan. Her work is regularly reviewed, and she herself is prominent as a reviewer, essayist, and commentator on American life and letters.

Nonetheless, Oates is not easily placed within critical contexts or among similar writers. She is not recognized for postmodernist perspectives and technical innovation as are Nabokov, Barth, Pynchon, Gass, Barthelme, and Vonnegut; not beloved and avidly read as are other women writers, such as Atwood, Morrison, Walker, Tyler, Didion, and Godwin; not accorded the respect given a host of male Jewish intellectual novelists, including Roth, Mailer, Singer, Bellow, and Doctorow; not seen within identifiable regional traditions as are Welty, Styron, Taylor, and Penn Warren; not as consistently popular with mass audiences as are King, Vidal, Heller, Kesey, Wolfe, Irving, Salinger, and Updike.

She is unique, alone, one of a kind—although her work is absolutely enriched by American experience, American culture, American intellectual and literary traditions. While exceedingly erudite and a formidable intellectual in her own right, Oates is most often categorized and dismissed as a popular writer with a penchant for the sensational and for the seamy side of life.

A serious critic of Oates's work is still a pioneer, charting one of the first maps of a largely unknown, unexplored, spacious, and expanding territory. In many ways the dialogue of Oatesian scholars takes place within a marginalized, sparsely populated corner of academia; our discourse is protracted over time and seldom interactive. Our subject is elusive, protean, moving off ahead of us into new territory. Not only is it hard to place Oates now; it is also hard to predict the turns her work might take. To be sure, many in the academy believe that it is premature to attempt to place a living author at all, that efforts to do so are doomed to failure, that the critical perspective of time is lacking. Be that as it may, I think we should try to understand the phenomenon of Joyce Carol Oates. I agree with Anne Tyler that "a hundred years from now people will laugh at us for sort of taking her for granted" (McCombs, C11).

The four book-length studies of Oates published at the end of the seventies (by Grant, Waller, Friedman, and Creighton) were each written separately, in isolation from one another, and so did not profit from dialogue and exchange: each picked up a different strand of Oates's work, and each established somewhat different and sometimes contradictory critical frameworks for discussion of it.

In the conclusion of my 1979 book I suggested that sometimes the subject and the form, as well as the emotional and the intellectual levels, of Oates's work seem disjunctive, and this blurs the implicit rhetoric. Readers of *them* (1969) don't know, for example, how to read the language of spiritual rebirth surrounding Jules Wendall's role in the Detroit riot; is his violent liberation treated positively or ironically or both? Similarly, are the compulsive sexual relationships of Oates's fiction potentially liberating experiences, sharing affinities with Lawrence's baptism of fire in passion, or are they more appropriately viewed as "a delirium and a pathological condition" making "of the lover a crazed man; his blood leaps with bacteria that shoots the temperature up toward death" (*T*, 274)? How should we view the pervasive violence, obsession, emotional duress of Oates's characters? Are these troubled, neurotic, violent, restless, antisocial characters deluded dreamers beating against intractable limitations, or are they ripe for liberation, struggling to grow?

As if to validate my concerns about ambiguities of affect on readers of Oates's work, two other studies—G. F. Waller's *Dreaming America: Obsession and Transcendence in the Fiction of Joyce Carol Oates* (1979) and Ellen Friedman's *Joyce Carol Oates* (1980)—articulate antithetical critical positions on this matter. Both place Oates's work within the same context— "the pervasive idealism of American culture, the romance tradition of classic American literature, and the quintessential American notion of freedom and self-sufficiency." Both see at the heart of Oates's work "the hunger to overcome limitations,"[3] to break out of confinements—to in some manner achieve the American dream of a renewed, better, fuller, or higher life. What is startling is how sharply these studies seem to differ on what Oates's work implies about this quest.

Whereas Waller argues that Oates's work is about the possibilities of transcendence, Friedman insisted it is about the necessity of limitations. Whereas Waller characterizes "Oates's aesthetic, in so far as we can talk of one, [as] . . . so clearly a neo-romantic celebration and evocation of flux and the human potential of unpredictability,"[4] Friedman characterizes Oates as an "inveterate antiromantic" whose fiction centers on the deflation of deluded Faustian overreachers, solipsistic dreamers, and the American Dream itself: "For Oates the American Dream is a false dream of conquest, control, ownership, and finally an impossible dream of overcoming mutability" (Friedman, 177).

Yet another voice in this implicit debate, this dialogue taking place in separate volumes, is Mary Kathryn Grant's, whose book *The Tragic Vision of Joyce Carol Oates* (1978) brings into play a somewhat different framework. Looking at Oates's extensive critical commentary on tragedy, Grant insists that Oates is "firmly rooted in the tradition of tragedy, in the belief in the self which struggles to achieve personality and identity and to transcend."[5] Essentially, Grant's position is somewhere between Waller's and Friedman's. She believes that Oates shows the limitations of "unheroic human beings" in a "leveled" world, yet that her intent is to articulate a vision of transcendence. Oates portrays "the hope of a hope" that "more than merely 'getting through,' more than just holding together the thousand pieces of one's life, her promised vision will point the way, for those who possess a tragic vision, toward finding a shape for so much pain" (Grant, 125). The vision of transcendence, in other words, will be supplied by the author rather than achieved by her "tragically diminished" characters.

All four of these early critical studies find Oates's essays revealing indexes to her fiction. Waller aptly calls Oates's first two volumes of essays, *The Edge of Impossibility: Tragic Forms in Literature* (1972) and *New Heaven, New Earth: The Visionary Experience in Literature* (1974), "prophetic" and notes her strong affinities with D. H. Lawrence. Relatively early in her career, Oates makes boldly prophetic statements about the state of our culture; she places the human personality in expansive historical and cultural contexts.

Finding us at the end of an era, Oates argues in these essays that the gradual transformation of Western consciousness is taking place, that the myth of the unique, proud, isolated entity of the self is being overthrown. Oates locates the "myth of the isolated self" in the I and not-I dualism that has dominated Western thought for centuries. This myth, rooted in the Renaissance's elevation of noble man over nature, continued in the romantic period with the exaltation of the subjective consciousness and is present in modern-day existentialism, in which man creates himself out of his own consciousness in an indifferent, hostile, or absurd universe. Oates argues that Freudian psychology has perpetuated this myth in the dialectics of the id and the ego and the equation of mental health with the ego's dominion over the id.

A key essay in the articulation of Oates's position is "The Death Throes of Romanticism: The Poetry of Sylvia Plath." Oates portrays Plath as "one of the last romantics," clinging with "gradually accelerating hysteria" to the "once-vital Renaissance ideal of subject/object antagonism." She claims that "Sylvia Plath acted out in her poetry and in her private life the deathliness of an old consciousness, the old corrupting hell of the Renaissance ideal and its 'I'-ness, separate and distinct from all other fields of consciousness."[6]

While both Friedman and Waller stress Oates's repudiation of conquering, masculine "I"-ness, Friedman seems to imply that Oates repudiates intelligence, consciousness, and the quest for meaning as well. On the contrary, Oates argues that Sylvia Plath, in portraying only the darkness of her own personality, only her ego's dissolution, tragically diminished her own superior intellect and failed to see "that the 'I' of the poet belongs as naturally in the universe as any other aspect of its fluid totality, above all that this 'I' exists in a field of living spirit of which it is one aspect" ("Plath," 140).

Friedman is quite right in noting that Oates frequently portrays narcissistic or Faustian overreachers, characters who with bloated egos try to incorporate the world into their selves, to manipulate, to control, to substitute themselves for the world. This kind of hubris attaches itself potently to the American dream of aspiration and self-actualization. American dreamers, Oates contends, are particularly susceptible to "the erecting of gigantic paranoid-delusion systems that are self-enclosed and self-destructing."[7] They are self-destructing because they presume that the human ego is "the supreme form of consciousness in the universe" and fail to account for the "otherness" they exclude: the nonrational side of personality, other people, an implacable, indifferent natural world.

Friedman also emphasizes another problem with manifestations of the American aspiring spirit, as it expresses itself in American culture: that aspiration easily becomes corrupted by materialism. Success becomes defined as the acquisition of wealth and position and possession. The emptiness and spiritual bankruptcy of this materialistic ideal are portrayed repeatedly in Oates's fiction, most potently in *Expensive People, Bellefleur*, and *American Appetites*.

Yet not all attempts in Oates's fiction to overcome human limitations are deluded; not all aspiration and all uses of intelligence and cunning are flawed. The writer herself is an ambitious, aspiring artist who does not scorn Faustian control in her own work. When accepting the National Book Award in Fiction for *them,* she noted:

The artists of America must resist the temptation to give up the struggle for consciousness, to go down with this age. It is very tempting for us, the disavowal of intelligence, this sub-religious gesture of surrender to the senses and emotions, to death. . . . Writers, trying to make sense of the age, are also creating it, and there is more need than ever for the contemplative life, for an assessment of where we are going and where we have come from. We need to withdraw from the age, to make ourselves detached. The writer of prose is committed to re-creating the world through language, and he should not be distracted from this task by even the most attractive of temptations. The opposite of language is silence; silence for human beings is death.[8]

The assessment of the age that the artist seeks to provide, the re-creation of the world through language, finds its parallels in fictional characters' attempts to understand, to gain some measure of control, to transcend limitations. The aspiring American spirit remains, I believe, a fundamental subject of Oates's fiction, and in this she remains within the tradition of American idealism and romanticism.

Thus, as I hope has been evident throughout this volume, I find more credence in Waller's assessment of Oates as a "neo-romantic" than in Friedman's characterization of her as an "inveterate antiromantic." Nevertheless, I think each critic has noted an important dimensions of Oates's fiction. We need a new term to encapsulate Oates's unique doubleness, her attraction to Blakean contraries, and her allegiance to, and skepticism about, the romantic tradition. I suggest the term *postmodern romantic*. Instead of the old stable ego, she depicts the Borgesian self, "the I, which doesn't exist." Yet this problematic self is everything. The paradoxical nature of the self—its simultaneous centrality and elusiveness—lies at the very heart of Oates's thought, complicating any simple view of her work and sometimes causing an ambiguity of affect for readers.

"The I, which doesn't exist," the human psyche, is made up of both conscious and unconscious contents, both a day and a night side. Part of the phantasmagoria of being human is being open to both sides and maintaining some equilibrium, some balance, through the inevitable changes and upheavals that will characterize one's life. Balance and equilibrium are not to be achieved through any simple imposition of limits or community values, as Friedman seems to imply. To stress these limits or values is to underplay the raggy edges of Oates's fictive world, its seething undercurrents, its vivid portrayals of "the human soul caught in the stampede of time,"[9] its rendering of the fluidity, fragility, and latent violence in the human personality. Often, an opening up to the night side of the self is essential. The passionate eruptions of the instinctual self are risky; they can unhinge the whole orderly structure of life. But an attempt to repress the pulsating human spirit is worse. It is the vulnerability and volatility of personality that make possible its growth toward self-actualization.

The ideal of permanence is deceptive; one cannot simply repeat the patterns of the past. Many of Oates's characters are so radically dislocated that accepting prescribed structures is quite beside the point: they literally need to chart a route, to make themselves anew. Jesse Harte, for example, is a literal and symbolic orphan at the start of *Wonderland*; his father has destroyed his entire family. He has no choice but to try to construct an identity within his horrific milieu.

Moreover, Oates's characters are not relieved of the burden of selfhood, although some would like to be. In Oates's early work, many of her female characters try to live in a vacuous void, try to put up walls around the emptiness, try to protect themselves from experience within conventional structures such as marriage. But such structures are shown to be inadequate defenses against the unpredictability of life.

Another way to avoid selfhood, individuation, is through mysticism. Stephen Petrie in *The Assassins,* for example, attempts to live in a dreamy mystical realm where self and the world are undifferentiated. There he finds a defense against life in the flesh, against the turmoil of emotions. When Stephen is "one with God" he is placidly serene, but when Andrew dies he no longer has the luxury of his detachment. His devastating final revelation is of the implacability of the physical world, the indifference of God, and the necessity of living a human life.

The most extensive treatment of the luring attractiveness of mystical transcendence is the portrait of Nathanael (Nathan) Vickery in *Son of the Morning.* The quest for meaning, for the "absolute dream," takes its most extreme expression in that character's conviction that he is coequal to God: "Nathan Vickery, the Chosen One, was immortal: unkillable" (*SM,* 353). It is appropriate that this "paranoid delusion" be deflated in the characteristic Oatesian way: by a devastating epiphany in which God is reduced to a ravenous mouth. There is no Godhead apart from life itself; there is no Ionescoesque "dream of absolute truth, the dream that explained everything."[10]

Transcendence comes not from the futile or self-destructive pursuit of an otherworldly paradise but from the possibility of recognizing this world as a paradise. A Lawrencean "new heaven and new earth" can be perceived in seeing that "the eternal being is made 'real' realized only through the temporal," by reexperiencing the ordinary world as "totally new," seeing "the interior dimension of the sacred . . . the kind of absolute spiritual conversion we find recorded so often in history—the undesired, perhaps dreaded rearrangement of all prior thought."[11]

In contradistinction to the uncompromising hubris of Nathanael Vickery, whose tragedy is his error in thinking himself godlike, Oates's novels also record the momentary visionary experiences of oneness with the natural world. In *Childwold* the continuity of life force outside of ego consciousness is apprehended fitfully by characters in the novel. More playfully fanciful is Oates's depiction of unions with the life force in *Bellefleur;* Raphael and Jeremiah literally merge for a time into the One, partaking in its eternality. This life force can be perceived as beautiful; it can also be construed as ravenous, implacable, indifferent—life feeding on life, jaws devouring jaws. Oates's vision of the oneness of life is, for the most part, unsentimentalized.

Another way to transcend the self is through erotic love. Like her earlier fiction, Oates's novels of the middle years portray compulsive sexual attractions. Such "unholy loves" are sometimes genuinely ecstatic and liberating experiences, Lawrencean baptisms of fire in passion; such, for a time, is the relationship of Brigit Stott and Alexis Kessler in *Unholy Loves*. Brigit, like Elena in *Do With Me What You Will*, does experience a genuine rebirth through her sexual relationship with Alexis; she gets beyond control of the personal self to the experience of the unconscious, the other. Moreover, she recognizes the transitory nature of the union and eventually moves beyond her desire for Alexis, subliminating its passionate energy in her art. Sometimes in Oates's fiction, however, the compulsions of sexual attraction are pathological and hallucinogenic delusions, treated with satire and wit, as in the portrait of Edwin Locke, the besotted insurance executive of *Cybele*, who deludes himself into thinking that authentic experience is achieved through a series of increasingly degrading and ridiculous affairs.

Perhaps the most important kind of transcendence in Oates's fiction is that achieved through the artistic process. Beginning with Brigit in *Unholy Loves*, Oates portrays the dynamics of the artistic personality, its necessary openness to the dangerous but rich world of the unconscious, its negotiation of the conscious and unconscious self, its transmutation of art out of life. This is a subject to be explored again in *Solstice* and in *Marya: A Life*, and a subject Oates writes about in critical essays, in which (as I explain in chapter 1) she shows her allegiance to high-modernist notions about the transcending autonomy of the "sacred" text.

Yet another kind of transcendence is that of idealism, a focus of the novel *Angel of Light*, in which Oates picks up a dominant strain in American character and history. Maurice Halleck is a modern-day angel of light, with affinities with John Brown and Thoreau. Although a foolish and deluded man betrayed by his wife and friend, he embodies love, loyalty, justice, and goodness—values that would redeem the corrupted, self-absorbed personal ambition that Nick embodies and that constitute the American dream at its basest level.

In these four novels of her early middle years, then, Oates shows the hubris and delusion incipient in attempts to transcend limitations. But the aspiring human spirit is not always defeated; the visionary is not totally illusory. The self can open up to the One, the life force beyond the isolated ego. Through love, art, sexuality, and idealism, transcendence is possible; the American dream may be respiritualized.

Until 1980 Oates's fiction was characteristically grounded in the world of experiential reality. For this reason the series of novels, starting with *Bellefleur*, that fabulistically reimagine nineteenth-century genres is a surprising tour-de-force. To be sure, Oates's work has always been richly allusive, acknowledging openly its debt to literary and intellectual traditions. Moreover, Oates has throughout her adult live lived in an academic community, as Eileen Teper Bender has emphasized in her book, *Joyce Carol Oates: Artist in Residence.*

Bender's study is an important contribution to critical perspectives on Oates's work because it stresses Oates's deliberate grounding within the community of discourse of the university; her insatiable curiosity about history, culture, and art; her multiple roles as artist, critic, and reader; her openly assimilative, allusive, and revisionist fiction; her cultivation of "contraries," of opposing selves, of alternating "marriages and infidelities" with literary traditions and literary precursors. In short, Bender recognizes the extraordinary importance of Oates's academic residence. She reminds those who would forget that Oates is a serious intellectual, a committed woman of letters who insists on the "moral, social, and political role of the artist and the value of literature in our time" (Bender, xi).

Bellefleur, A Bloodsmoor Romance, and *Mysteries of Winterthurn* are especially literary: they call attention to their fictionality, invention, and artifice, to the fact that they are mediated through the academic mind of Joyce Carol Oates. And in their self-reflexiveness rather than mimetic representation, they resemble postmodernist works of other writers. But clearly, Oates's intention is to use the prismatic lens of these anachronistic genres to present a serious study of American character, American society, and the American dream.

Oates importantly clarifies the encompassing range of her realistic technique: "My method has always been to combine the 'naturalistic' world with the 'symbolic' method of expression, so that I am always—or usually—writing about real people in real society, but the means of expression may be naturalistic, realistic, surreal, or parodic. In this way I have, to my own satisfaction at least, solved the old problem—should one be faithful to the 'real' world, or to one's imagination?"[12] *Bellefleur,* says the author in a note to the volume, "is a work of the imagination, and must obey, with both humility and audacity, imagination's laws"—and indeed it does. It brings out explicitly what has always been implicit in Oates's method: her wide-ranging—sometimes straight, sometimes ironic and playful—use of traditional narrative forms and the intellectual heritage of Western, and especially American, culture.

Oates's work is, then, considerably more various than she is usually given credit for. But she is "traditional" in her consistent allegiance to the humanistic aims of literature rather than to technique itself. I agree with Greg

Johnson, who writes in *Understanding Joyce Carol Oates* (1987) that "her versatility as a fiction writer relates directly to her overwhelming fascination with the phenomenon of contemporary America: its colliding social and economic forces, its philosophical contradictions, its wayward, often violent energies. . . . all of her characters, regardless of background, suffer intensely the conflicts and contradictions at the heart of our culture."[13]

Bellefleur is a highly imaginative rendition of these conflicts and contradictions. The novel is what Oates has called "a complex parable of American aspirations and tragic shortcomings." It picks up on certain strains in the American dream and character—the quest for willful acquisition and the quest for spiritual transcendence, impulses acted out in the two sides of the family. Importantly, as in so many of Oates's more realistic novels as well, both quests can be egotistical, disrespectful denials of the other represented in other people and in nature. Moreover, these dual impulses illustrate the "divided stream" of American culture, observed by Charles Child Walcutt in *American Literary Naturalism* (1956)—the splitting of the American dream into separate material and spiritual dimensions. While Jedediah attempts to retreat from the world of harsh competitiveness and to contemplate the face of God, he is forced to get back into the human community: one cannot retreat from life any more than one can, like Gideon and Leah and all their monomaniacal precursors, impose one's will on it.

The second book in this series, *A Bloodsmoor Romance,* is also ultimately about "conflicts and contradictions at the heart of our culture" and incorporates a portrayal of a tenacious instinct for survival and self-determination. Oates's reimaginings of nineteenth-century genres expose their misogynistic underpinnings and the stridently patriarchal foundations of turn-of-the-century American culture. Played off against the egomania of Zinn and his mad science are the fates of his five daughters, who are literally and figuratively confined within the domestic sphere and within the restrictive and prescriptive roles dictated by the patriarchy. Influenced by contemporary feminist scholarship, Oates develops ribald and caustic subtexts, escapist strategies both deliberately and fortuitously employed by the Zinn sisters. The novel demonstrates a tenacious degree of female self-determination to transcend limitations despite the most formidable of obstacles to female selfhood.

Finally, *Mysteries of Winterthurn* deals with the dark, "invisible" side of the patriarchy, a darkness connected with women and with crimes against women. The way toward freedom and self-determination here has an especially disturbing side. Perdita exacts revenge on the patriarchal order, it appears, by drawing Xavier into her dark world and plotting the murder of her husband, his mother, and his mistress. In so doing she is saved from perdition and liberated into normal domesticity. Perdita, whom Oates has called "an unregenerate murderess" (Preface to *MW*, 376) demonstrates a tenacious instinct for survival. Oates's solution to Perdita's entrapment is as disturbing as the misogynistic and stereotypical views of women in our cultural and historical heritage are virulent.

The heightened concern with feminist perspectives in these experimental novels is also evident in Oates's critical writing and her recent realistic fiction. In her prophetic voice, Oates suggests that the devaluing of woman is part of a now-anachronistic "point in civilization [when] this very masculine, combative ideal of an 'I' set against all other 'I's'—and against nature as well—was necessary in order to wrench man from the hermetic contemplation of a God-centered universe and get him into action, it is no longer necessary, its health has become a pathology" ("Plath," 119). Furthermore, she argues that a "man's quarrel with Woman is his quarrel with himself—with those 'despised' and muted elements in his personality which he cannot freely acknowledge because they challenge his sense of masculine supremacy and control" ("At Least," 35).

Indeed, Eileen Teper Bender sees affinities between Oates's fictional technique and recent examples and articulations of a female aesthetic. Women's art is said to be "weblike," "inclusive," less concerned with object and product than with "growth, proliferation, and evolution." Bender characterizes Oates's fiction of the last decade as a feminist art "of assemblage, revisable, in motion, fluid as cinema, eccentric and various as a crazy quilt." So too does she note that the "permeability of codes, conventions, and boundaries . . . at the heart of Oates's work" is in keeping with a feminist aesthetic (Bender, 180, 182). Oates's very identity as an "artist in residence," in fact, displays a similar permeability of the roles of the artistic and the academic, a merging of literary and extraliterary influences. Whether or not one sees Oates's synthesizing of various roles and influences as peculiarly feminist or not, it is true that she is centrally concerned with the pathological bifurcations of our culture, and that often these divisions exist along stereotypical gender lines.

The fundamental dividedness, of course, is within the human psyche itself, and Oates situates some of the drama of her later works within the warring dualities of female selfhood. For women as well as for men, authentic selfhood is to be achieved by balancing the contraries at the root of the problematics of being—conscious and unconscious, intellect and emotion, inner and outer, self and other.

Solstice, for example, is an unsentimentalized study of the contraries implicit in female friendship, selfhood, and creativity, played out in the relationship of Sheila and Monica. The novel details the subtle and sometimes surprising shifts of control and submission, dependency and dominance between them. They struggle to arrive at a solstice, an equilibrium, in a bond both visceral and quixotic. One woman is an artist, the other a teacher. At one level they are dual aspects of their creator; at another they are two halves of the self, vying for ascendancy and control and, ideally, balance.

Marya: A Life is about a young woman who tries to achieve selfhood, not through balance but through the suppression one side of her being. Lurking in her subconscious and associated with sexuality, weakness, rage, and madness is a dark double, her lost mother. Marya's life is a progressive strengthening of brittle self-sufficiency, a rejection of the inner "female" world of emotion for the outer "male" world of success. Yet at the end of the novel the implication is certainly that Marya must come to terms with her femaleness and her matrilineal heritage.

Finally, *You Must Remember This* depicts Enid Maria, whose "good" side is the reliable A student, the talented musician, the dutiful daughter, and the devout Catholic, and whose "bad" side is "Angel-face," the side that prods Enid into a dangerous flirtation and a passionate affair with her Uncle Felix, which ends badly. Yet Enid survives and prevails though the highs and lows of her relationship with Felix. Her talent, compassion, intelligence, and hope are the qualities of a survivor; so too are her Angel-face daring, passion, irreverence, skepticism, and willfulness. She achieves a workable balance of the dualities within her.

I wish particularly to stress Oates's respect for the stubborn, self-reliant, self-determining nature of her characters, both female and male. Despite the mysterious, protean, changeable nature of identity, they do instinctively presume that "the I, which doesn't exist, is everything." They, along with William James, take as their first act of freedom the belief in freedom. They tenaciously attempt to "forge their own souls by way of the choices they make, large and small, conscious and half-conscious" (Preface to *M,* 377). In this they are embodiments of the American spirit of individualism. Even the most repressed, the most victimized—even when they most painfully act out the central conflicts and contradictions of our culture—do not readily accept imposed barriers. In their tenacious will to be, in their attempt to transcend limitations, they are fundamentally American romantics.

An emblematic figure displaying the paradoxes and dynamics within

American romantic individualism is the boxer, a figure Oates studies in her book *On Boxing* as well as in a number of critical and occasional essays. Boxing is a stripped-down version of the struggle to survive, making "visible what is invisible in us," serving as "a reading of American experience, unsentimentalized and graphic."

Boxing dramatizes in graphically physical terms the mysterious dynamics of the self. Boxers attempt to arrive at "the outermost limits of their beings; they will know, as few of us know, what physical and psychic power they possess—of how much, or how little, they are capable" (*OB*, 8). Boxing is about the triumphant or defeated human will. Nothing happens in the ring that is not a product of the boxer's will or failure of will. To box is to attempt to transcend pain and to transform it into its polar opposite. And in this willful transformation of pain and conflict into achievement and triumph, the boxer is like the writer, who in a different realm is also absorbed with the "fascination of what's difficult," and who also constantly seeks to reestablish "the parameters of one's being" (*OB*, 26).

An analogous attempt to extend those parameters for Joyce Carol Oates is her assumption of the pseudonym Rosamond Smith. Through using a pseudonym, says Oates, writers attempt "an interior and not merely an outward transformation, a conspicuous redefining of the self" ("Pseudo," 388). It is an attempt to be an other, and *Lives of the Twins*, and *Soul/Mate*, and *Nemesis*, the books written by Oates's other self, Rosamond Smith, are about characters obsessed with an other. Oates recognizes the deep drives within the human psyche, and especially within the artist, to break through narrow and rigid definitions of the self. Oates has attempted to gain for herself freedom from the oppressive public identity of "Joyce Carol Oates," freedom to be a genre writer, a producer of slick psychological thrillers. But now that the secret is out, that freedom is problematic: for better or worse, the writer is doomed to be perceived as Joyce Carol Oates, with all of the preconceptions attached to that name.

In her two most recent novels, *American Appetites* and *Because It Is Bitter, and Because It Is My Heart* Oates is prototypically herself, using the realistic mode that has been her dominant style and focusing on the themes and situations that have preoccupied her throughout her career. Even the structures of these novels, which each begin with a scene of catastrophic violence, follow a pattern that has been Oatesian from her very first novel, *With Shuddering Fall* (1964). *American Appetites* might be seen as a nonsatiric version of *Expensive People*, recording a scene of family violence amid the affluent, privileged, upper-middle-class world. Ian McCullough is a character type that has been portrayed many times before in Oates's fiction. *Because It Is Bitter, and Because It Is My Heart,* although it interjects a racial dimension into the conflict, recalls many other of Oates's novels, including *them,* with its portrayal of the survival tactics of a young girl and young man of the underclass, and *Childwold, Marya,* and *You Must Remember This,* with their depictions of adolescence and incipient intellectual awakening in the bleak cities and backcountry of Oates's Eden County.

Despite the imaginative richness of Oates's fictional world, in other words, there is an underlying repetitiveness. Oates is obsessed with the same subjects and situations, recast into new fictions. Her central obsession is with the search for authentic individuality. She recognizes that the old stable ego is a fiction; rather, the personality is a fragile, protean, passionate, mysterious entity, precariously balanced between conscious and unconscious contents. Oates respects the other within the self, other people, and the natural world. She depicts the need to get beyond the conflicts and contradictions in our culture that would deny authentic selfhood, and she portrays the enormous difficulty of that task.

The way toward fulfillment is not through a repudiation of one's culture. Oates's portrayals of characters who attempt radical alternatives, who attempt to cut themselves off from an engaged role in ordinary life—Stephen Petrie, Nathanael Vickery, Jedediah Bellefleur—are all tinged with irony. Neither can one choose not to play the games of the social masquerade, like Ian McCullough in *American Appetites.* While characters like Ian reach a despairing dead end in the quest for meaning, Oates does not. Her role is to catalogue his pain, not necessarily to share in it. In most of her novels, such as her most recent, *Because It Is Bitter, and Because It Is My Heart,* she portrays characters who despite embittering experiences retain a tenacious will to endure and a restless human spirit.

But the complexity of Oates's fictional world, with its implicit, inchoate contraries, needs to be experienced rather than necessarily interpreted, assessed, and understood: "The formal artist is one who arranges his dreams into a shape that can be experienced by other people. There is no guarantee that art will be understood, not even by the artist; it is not meant to be understood but experienced" (Oates quoted in Parini, 160). What one experiences in reading Oates's canon is a sense of a buoyant and sustaining intelligence, creativity, and spirit. Her works are hugely ambitious; she mocks but does not discredit her laughably Balzacian hunger "to put the whole world in a book."[14] She is critical of the egomania of the Western tragic and romantic traditions, but she does not repudiate their human-centeredness. She sees her works, and all art, as a type of human triumph, a transmutation of obsession and pain and discipline into "a kind of massive, joyful experiment done with words . . . submitted to one's peers for judgement."[15]

The judgment must be that Joyce Carol Oates is a very impressive woman of letters. Her novels and critical essays alone are a major achievement; I have not had space in this study to consider what has continued to be her métier, short-story craftsmanship, or to discuss her poetry, drama, reviews, and occasional work. Her important place in American literary and intellectual history is assured. Moreover, it may well be that her work has only begun. I look forward to the continued unfolding of her extraordinarily rich and productive career.

Notes and References

Preface

1. John Barth, "The Literature of Replenishment," *Atlantic Monthly,* January 1980, 66.
2. Preface to *Mysteries of Winterthurn,* in *(Woman) Writer: Occasions and Opportunities* (New York: Dutton, 1988), 313; hereafter cited in the text as Preface to *MW.*
3. "Mike Tyson," in *(Woman) Writer,* 231.
4. Joe David Bellamy, ed., "The Dark Lady of American Letters: An Interview with Joyce Carol Oates," *Atlantic,* February 1972, 63–67, reprinted in *Conversations with Joyce Carol Oates,* 17–27.
5. Letter to the author, 16 July 1990.

Chapter One

1. "Does the Writer Exist?," in *(Woman) Writer,* 48; hereafter cited in the text as "Exist."
2. "My Father, My Fiction," *New York Times Magazine,* 19 March 1989, 45; hereafter cited in the text as "Father."
3. Preface to *Marya: A Life,* in *(Woman) Writer,* 376–77 (hereafter cited in the text as "Preface to *M*"); "Beginnings," in *(Woman) Writer,* 19–21 (hereafter cited in the text as "Beginnings").
4. *On Boxing* (Garden City, N.Y.: Dolphin / Doubleday, 1987), 72; hereafter cited in the text as *OB.*
5. "Budapest Journal: May 1980," in *(Woman) Writer,* 330; hereafter cited in the text as "Budapest."
6. Her brother Fred, called "Robin," was born in 1943. There is also a younger sister Lynn, born in 1956, who is autistic and has been institutionalized since early adolescence ("Father," 80).
7. Preface to *You Must Remember This,* in *(Woman) Writer,* 379; hereafter cited in the text as Preface to *Y.* Lockport gave her a "key" to the city in 1987 and held a festival in her honor in 1988 (David Germain, "Author Oates Tells Where She's Been, Where She's Going," *Lockport Union Sun & Journal,* 24 March 1988, reprinted in *Conversations with Joyce Carol Oates,* ed. Lee Milazzo [Jackson: University Press of Mississippi, 1989]; hereafter cited in the text as Germain).
8. "Visions of Detroit," in *(Woman) Writer,* 348; hereafter cited in the text as "Detroit."
9. Letter to Dale Boesky, "Correspondence with Miss Joyce Carol Oates,"

121

International Review of Psychoanalysis 2 (1975): 482; hereafter cited in the text as Boesky.

10. *Childwold* (New York: Vanguard Press, 1976), 290; hereafter cited in the text as *C.*

11. John Updike, "What You Deserve Is What You Get," review of *You Must Remember This, New Yorker,* 28 December 1987, 119.

12. "Pleasure, Duty, Redemption Then and Now: Susan Warner's *Diana,*" in *(Woman) Writer,* 191; hereafter cited in the text as "Pleasure."

13. "The Dream of the 'Sacred Text,'" in *(Woman) Writer,* 43; hereafter cited in the text as "Dream."

14. Introduction to *The Profane Art: Essays and Reviews* (New York: Dutton, 1983), 2.

15. Letter to the author, 22 October 1975.

16. "Against Nature," in *(Woman) Writer,* 75.

17. "'Soul *at the White Heat*'": The Romance of Emily Dickinson's Poetry," in *(Woman) Writer,* 185; hereafter cited in the text as "Soul."

18. "Wonderlands," in *(Woman) Writer,* 79–105.

19. Preface to *(Woman) Writer,* xii.

20. "Looking for Thoreau," in *(Woman) Writer,* 155.

21. Preface to *Bellefleur,* in *(Woman) Writer,* 371; hereafter cited in the text as Preface to *B.*

Chapter Two

1. Introduction to *The Edge of Impossibility: Tragic Forms in Literature* (New York: Vanguard Press, 1972), 8.

2. Quoted in Judith Applebaum, "Joyce Carol Oates," *Publishers Weekly* 26 (June 1978), 12–13, reprinted in *Conversations with Joyce Carol Oates,* 60.

3. Oates's review of *The Simone Weil Reader,* ed. George A. Panichas. *New Republic* 177 (2 July 1977), 33–37.

4. *Son of the Morning* (New York: Vanguard Press, 1978), 76; hereafter cited in the text as *SM.*

5. *them* (Greenwich, Conn.: Fawcett Crest, 1970), 255; hereafter cited in the text as *T.*

6. "New Heaven and New Earth," *Saturday Review* 55 (4 November 1972), 53; hereafter cited in the text as "New."

7. Quoted in Robert Phillips, "Joyce Carol Oates: The Art of Fiction LXXII," *Paris Review* 20 (Fall 1978), 199–226, reprinted in *Conversations with Joyce Carol Oates,* 81, 70. Hereafter cited in the text as Phillips.

8. "The Nature of Short Fiction: or, The Nature of My Short Fiction," Oates's preface to *Handbook of Short Story Writing,* ed. Frank A. Dickson and Sandra Smythe (New York: Writer's Digest Books, 1970), xii.

9. *Unholy Loves* (New York: Vanguard Press, 1979), 258; hereafter cited in the text as *UL.*

10. "The Short Story," *Southern Humanities Review* 5 (Summer 1971): 213–14.

11. *Cybele* (Santa Barbara, Calif.: Black Sparrow Press, 1979), 67; hereafter cited in the text as *C*.

12. Linda W. Wagner, "Oates' *Cybele*," *Notes on Contemporary Literature* 5, no. 2 (November 1981): 2–8, suggests that Edwin Locke can be read "as an ironic re-creation of seventeenth century philosopher, John Locke, creator of the pleasure principle."

13. See E. O. James, *The Cult of the Mother Goddess: An Archaeological and Documentary Study* (London: Thames and Hudson, 1959), 161–91.

14. Such as Jonathan Williams, "That Old Original Phrygian Ball-Buster," in *An Ear in Bartram's Tree: Selected Poems: 1957–1967* (Chapel Hill: University of North Carolina Press, 1969); Basil Bunting, "Attis: Or, Something Missing," in *Collected Poems* (New York: Oxford University Press, 1978), p. 8.

15. *A Moveable Feast:* Interviews and Readings on Audiotape (Columbia, Mo.: American Audio Prose Library, 1982).

16. *Angel of Light* (New York: Dutton, 1981), 58, 59; hereafter cited in the text as *AL*.

Chapter Three

1. Oates now says that there are five novels in all, including a fifth called *My Heart Laid Bare:* "Those earlier books are not romantic. They're what could be called post-modernist and experimental. I'm going back to that mode, maybe in 1990. I have two more novels in that series" (quoted in Germain, 178).

2. Letter to the author, 27 June 1990.

3. Quoted in Leif Sjoberg, "An Interview with Joyce Carol Oates," *Contemporary Literature* 23, no. 3 (Summer 1982), 269–89, reprinted in *Conversations with Joyce Carol Oates,* 116; hereafter cited in the text as Sjoberg.

4. Jean-Francois Lyotard, *The Postmodern Condition: A Report on Knowledge,* trans. Geoff Bennington and Brian Massumi (Minneapolis: University of Minnesota Press, 1984).

5. Joyce Carol Oates, *Bellefleur* (New York: Dutton, 1980); hereafter cited in the text as *B*.

6. Eileen Teper Bender, *Joyce Carol Oates, Artist in Residence* (Bloomington and Indianapolis: Indiana University Press, 1987), 111; hereafter cited in the text as Bender.

7. "The Strange Real World," review of *Bellefleur, New York Times Book Review,* 20 July 1980, 1, 21.

8. Joyce Carol Oates, *A Bloodsmoor Romance* (New York: Dutton, 1982), 207; hereafter cited in the text as *BR*.

9. The novel is dedicated to Elaine Showalter, Oates's Princeton colleague and friend, who has written *A Literature of Their Own: British Women Novelists from Brontë to Lessing* (Princeton, N.J.: Princeton University Press, 1977).

10. Letter to the author, 16 July 1990.

11. "'At Least I Have Made a Woman of Her': Images of Women in Yeats, Lawrence, Faulkner," *The Profane Art,* 35. Hereafter cited in the text as "At Least."

12. Sandra M. Gilbert and Susan Gubar, "Sex Wars: Not the Fun Kind," *New York Times Book Review,* 27 December 1987, 1.

13. *Mysteries of Winterthurn* (New York: Dutton, 1984), 103; hereafter cited in the text as *MW.*

14. "Un-Tricking the Eye: Joyce Carol Oates and the Feminist Ghost Story," *Arizona Quarterly* 41, no. 1 (Spring 1985): 5–23.

15. Linda Kuehl, ed., "An Interview with Joyce Carol Oates," *Commonweal* 91 (5 December 1969): 307–18, reprinted in *Conversations with Joyce Carol Oates,* p. 9.

16. *The Madwoman in the Attic: The Woman Writer and the Nineteenth-Century Literary Imagination* (New Haven: Yale University Press, 1980).

Chapter Four

1. "Unliberated Women in Joyce Carol Oates's Fiction," *World Literature Written in English* 17, no. 1 (April 1978): 165–75, reprinted in *Critical Essays on Joyce Carol Oates,* ed. Linda Wagner (Boston: G. K. Hall, 1979), 149–56.

2. See, for example, "(Woman) Writer: Theory and Practice," in *(Woman) Writer,* 22–32. Hereafter cited in the text as "Woman."

3. Joyce Carol Oates, *Solstice* (New York: Dutton, 1985), 5. Hereafter cited in the text as *S.*

4. *A Room of One's Own* (New York: Harcourt Brace, 1957), 86–88.

5. *The Reproduction of Mothering: Psychoanalysis and the Sociology of Gender* (Berkeley: University of California Press, 1978), 93, 200.

6. Phil McCombs, "The Demonic Imagination of Joyce Carol Oates," *Washington Post,* 18 August 1986, C11. Hereafter cited in the text as McCombs.

7. Joyce Carol Oates, *Marya: A Life* (New York: Dutton, 1986), 5. Hereafter cited in the text as *M.*

8. Elaine Showalter has commented, "The community of women is not idyllic, but torn by rage, competition, primal jealousies, ambiguous desire, and emotional violence, just like the world in which women seem subordinate to and victimized by men. And we do not know what kind of renewal Marya's reunion with her mother will bring. . . . The mother's country may be a wilderness rather than a peaceful or paradisal garden; yet to refuse or to deny it is to be in permanent exile." ("My Friend, Joyce Carol Oates: An Intimate Portrait," *Ms. Magazine* [March 1986], 44–50, reprinted in *Conversations with Joyce Carol Oates,* 134).

9. Joyce Carol Oates, *You Must Remember This* (New York: Dutton, 1987), 36. Hereafter cited in the text as *Y.*

10. "Lawrence's *Götterdämmerung:* The Tragic Vision of *Women in Love,*" *Critical Inquiry* 4 (Spring 1978): 564, reprinted, with new title, in *Contraries* (New York: Oxford University Press, 1981), 141–70.

Chapter Five

1. "Blood, Neon, and Failure in the Desert," *(Woman) Writer*, 264; hereafter cited in the text as "Blood."

2. "Golden Gloves," in *Last Days* (New York: Dutton, 1984), 69; hereafter cited in the text as "Gloves."

3. "Pseudonymous Selves," in *(Woman) Writer*, 33; hereafter cited in the text as "Pseudonymous."

4. Rosamond Smith, *Lives of the Twins* (New York: Simon and Schuster, 1987), 96; hereafter cited in the text as *LT*.

5. Edwin McDowell, "A Sad Joyce Carol Oates Forswears Pseudonyms," *New York Times*, 10 February 1987, N25, reprinted in *Conversations with Joyce Carol Oates*, 147–48. The article claims that Oates's attempt to publish under a pseudonym was a surprise to her agent, Blanche Gregory; to her editor at Dutton, William Abrahams; and to "Rosamond Smith's" editor at Simon and Schuster, Nancy Nicholas.

6. Rosamond Smith, *Soul/Mate* (New York: Dutton, 1989), 19; hereafter cited in the text as *S/M*.

7. "'Where Are You Going, Where Have You Been?' and *Smooth Talk*: Short Story into Film," *(Woman) Writer*, 317.

8. Rev. Stopford A. Brooke, introduction to Percy Bysshe Shelley, *Epipsychidion*, a type facsimile reprint of the original edition first published in 1821 (New York: AMS Press, 1975), xxiii.

9. Thomas McFarland, 62-year-old specialist in English romantic literature and holder of an endowed professorship at Princeton, was accused of making sexual advances to a male graduate student. He was suspended from his duties for the academic year 1988–89. In the summer of 1989, as the controversy surrounding the incident and the university's handling of it continued to brew on campus and in the newspapers, McFarland took an early retirement. Oates appears to have conflated this incident with a spate of murders and attempted murders in Princeton, New Jersey, around the same time.

10. Rosamond Smith, *Nemesis* (New York: Dutton, 1990), 4; hereafter cited in the text as *N*.

11. Quoted in Jay Parini, "My Writing Is Full of Lives I Might Have Led," *Boston Globe Magazine*, 2 August 1987, reprinted in *Conversations with Joyce Carol Oates*, 159.

Chapter Six

1. Joyce Carol Oates, *American Appetites* (New York: Dutton, 1989), 116; hereafter cited in the text as *AA*.

2. "Murder She Wrote," review of *Because It Is Bitter, and Because It Is My Heart*, *Nation*, 2 July 1990, 27–29.

3. *Because It Is Bitter, and Because It Is My Heart* (New York: Dutton, 1990), 182; hereafter cited in the text as *BB*.

4. "The Black Riders," *Prose and Poetry* (New York: The Library of America, 1984), 1299.

5. "Bookmark," episode 214, discussion with the author about *Because It Is Bitter* (Louis Lapham, host), aired in New York, April 1990.

6. "Other Celebrity Voices: How Art Has Touched Our Lives," *Today's Health* 52 (May 1974), 31.

Chapter Seven

1. Quoted by Bruce F. Michelson in the preface to Francine Lercangée, *Joyce Carol Oates: An Annotated Bibliography* (New York: Garland, 1986), xiii.

2. Joyce Carol Oates, "Meeting the Gorbachevs," *(Woman) Writer*, 358.

3. Ellen G. Friedman, *Joyce Carol Oates* (New York: Ungar, 1980), 3, 196. Hereafter cited in the text as Friedman.

4. G. F. Waller, *Dreaming America: Obsession and Transcendence in the Fiction of Joyce Carol Oates* (Baton Rouge: Louisiana State University Press, 1979), 21. Hereafter cited in the text as Waller.

5. Mary Kathryn Grant, R.S.M., *The Tragic Vision of Joyce Carol Oates* (Durham, N.C.: Duke University Press, 1978), 118. Hereafter cited in the text as Grant.

6. This essay is collected in *New Heaven, New Earth: The Visionary Experience in Literature* (New York: Vanguard Press, 1974), 118–19. Hereafter cited in the text as "Plath."

7. Joyce Carol Oates, "Out of Stone, into Flesh: The Imagination of James Dickey," *New Heaven, New Earth*, 259–60.

8. *December Magazine* 12, nos. 1-2 (1970), 215.

9. Joyce Carol Oates, "The Nightmare of Naturalism: Harriette Arnow's *The Dollmaker*," *New Heaven, New Earth*, 105.

10. Oates's prefaces her volume of essays, *The Edge of Impossibility*, with a passage from Ionesco's *Fragments of a Journal*, from which this quote is taken. The book is a meditation on the tragic impossibility of the absolute dream.

11. Joyce Carol Oates, "The Hostile Sun: The Poetry of D. H. Lawrence," *New Heaven, New Earth*, 51, 56–57.

12. Ann Charters, ed., *The Story and its Writer* (New York: St. Martin's, 1983), 1081–82.

13. Greg Johnson, *Understanding Joyce Carol Oates* (Columbia, S.C.: University of South Carolina Press, 1987), 8.

14. Quoted in Walter Clemons, "Joyce Carol Oates: Love and Violence," *Newsweek*, 11 December 1972, 72.

15. Joyce Carol Oates, "The Myth of the Isolated Artist," *Psychology Today*, May 1973, 74.

Selected Bibliography

PRIMARY WORKS

Novels

American Appetites. New York: Dutton, 1989; New York: Harper & Row, 1990.
Angel of Light. New York: Dutton, 1981; New York: Warner, 1982.
The Assassins: A Book of Hours. New York: Vanguard, 1975; New York: Fawcett Crest, 1983.
Because It Is Bitter, and Because It Is My Heart. New York: Dutton, 1990.
Bellefleur. New York: Dutton, 1980; New York: Dutton/Obelisk, 1987.
A Bloodsmoor Romance. New York: Dutton, 1982; New York: Warner, 1983.
Childwold. New York: Vanguard, 1976; New York: Fawcett Crest, 1981.
Cybele. Santa Barbara: Black Sparrow Press, 1979; New York: Dutton/Obelisk, 1986.
Do With Me What You Will. New York: Vanguard, 1973; New York: Fawcett Crest, 1983.
Expensive People. New York: Vanguard, 1968; New York: Fawcett Crest, 1970, 1974, 1982.
A Garden of Earthly Delights. New York: Vanguard, 1967; Greenwich, Conn.: Fawcett Crest, 1969.
Marya: A Life. New York: Dutton, 1986; Boston: G. K. Hall, 1987 (large print); New York: Berkley, 1985.
Mysteries of Winterthurn. New York: Dutton, 1984; New York: Berkley, 1985.
Solstice. New York: Dutton, 1985; New York: Berkley, 1986.
Son of the Morning. New York: Vanguard Press, 1978; New York: Fawcett Crest, 1979.
them. New York: Vanguard, 1969; New York: Fawcett Crest, 1984.
Unholy Loves. New York: Vanguard, 1979; New York: Fawcett Crest, 1984.
With Shuddering Fall. New York: Vanguard, 1964; Greenwich, Conn.: Fawcett Crest, 1971.
Wonderland. New York: Vanguard, 1971; Greenwich, Conn.: Fawcett Crest, 1973.
You Must Remember This. New York: Dutton, 1987; New York: Harper & Row, 1988.

Novels by Rosamond Smith (Pseudonym)

Lives of the Twins. New York: Simon and Schuster, 1987.

Nemesis. New York: Dutton, 1990.
Soul/Mate. New York: Dutton, 1989.

Short Story Collections and Novella

All the Good People I've Left Behind. Santa Barbara, Calif.: Black Sparrow Press, 1979.

The Assignation. New York: Ecco Press, 1988; New York: Harper & Row, 1989.

By the North Gate. New York: Vanguard, 1963; Greenwich, Conn.: Fawcett, 1971.

Crossing the Border: Fifteen Tales. New York: Vanguard, 1976; New York: Fawcett Crest, 1983.

The Goddess and Other Women. New York: Vanguard, 1974; Greenwich, Conn.: Fawcett Crest, 1976.

The Hungry Ghosts: Seven Allusive Comedies. Los Angeles: Black Sparrow Press, 1974.

Last Days. New York: Dutton, 1984; New York: Dutton/Obelisk, 1986.

Marriages and Infidelities. New York: Vanguard, 1972; Greenwich, Conn.: Fawcett Crest, 1973.

Night-Side: Eighteen Tales. New York: Vanguard, 1977; New York: Fawcett Crest, 1984.

The Poisoned Kiss and Other Stories from the Portuguese. Fernandes/Joyce Carol Oates. New York: Vanguard, 1975.

Raven's Wing. New York: Dutton, 1986; New York: Dutton/Obelisk, 1987.

The Seduction and Other Stories. Los Angeles: Black Sparrow Press, 1975; New York: Dutton/Obelisk, 1987.

A Sentimental Education: Stories. New York: Dutton, 1980; New York: Dutton/ Obelisk, 1982.

The Triumph of the Spider Monkey Santa Barbara, Calif.: Black Sparrow Press, 1976; New York: Fawcett Crest, 1976. Novella.

Upon the Sweeping Flood and Other Stories. New York: Vanguard, 1966; Greenwich, Conn.: Fawcett Crest, 1971.

The Wheel of Love and Other Stories. New York: Vanguard, 1970; Greenwich, Conn.: Fawcett Crest, 1972.

Where Are You Going, Where Have You Been? Stories of Young America. Greenwich, Conn.: Fawcett Crest, 1974. Reprinted stories.

Wild Saturday and Other Stories. London: Dent, 1984. Reprints of selected stories from other collections.

Collected Essays

Contraries: Essays. New York: Oxford University Press, 1981.

The Edge of Impossibility: Tragic Forms in Literature. New York: Vanguard, 1972; Greenwich, Conn.: Fawcett Premier, 1973.

New Heaven, New Earth: The Visionary Experience in Literature. New York: Vanguard, 1974; New York: Fawcett Crest, 1978.

On Boxing. Garden City, N.Y.: Dolphin/Doubleday, 1987; New York: Zebra Books, 1988.

The Profane Art: Essays and Reviews. New York: Dutton, 1983; New York: Persea Books, n.d.

(Woman) Writer: Occasions and Opportunities. New York: Dutton, 1988; New York: Dutton/Obelisk, 1989.

Poetry Collections

Angel Fire: Poems. Baton Rouge: Louisiana State University Press, 1973.

Anonymous Sins and Other Poems. Baton Rouge: Louisiana State University Press, 1969.

Dreaming America & Other Poems. New York: Aloe Editions, 1973.

The Fabulous Beasts: Poems. Baton Rouge: Louisiana State University Press, 1975.

Invisible Women: New and Selected Poems, 1970–1982. Princeton, N.J.: Ontario Review Press, 1982.

Love and Its Derangements: Poems. Baton Rouge: Louisiana State University Press, 1970.

Season of Peril. Santa Barbara: Black Sparrow Press, 1977.

The Time Traveler: Poems 1983–1989. New York: Dutton, 1989.

Women in Love and Other Poems. New York: Albondocani Press, 1968.

Women Whose Lives Are Food, Men Whose Loves Are Money: Poems. Baton Rouge: Louisiana State University Press, 1978.

Volumes of Plays

Miracle Play. Los Angeles: Black Sparrow Press, 1974.

Three Plays. Princeton: Ontario Review Press, 1980. Contains "Ontological Proof of My Existence," "Miracle Play," "The Triumph of the Spider Monkey."

Edited Volumes

The Best American Short Stories 1979: Selected from US and Canadian Magazines. Edited by Joyce Carol Oates with Shannon Ravenel. Boston: Houghton Mifflin, 1979.

First Person Singular. Princeton, N.J.: Ontario Review Press, 1982. Previously published interviews compiled by Oates.

Night Walks: A Bedside Companion. Princeton, N.J.: Ontario Review Press, 1982. Stories compiled by Oates.

Reading the Fights. Edited by Joyce Carol Oates with Daniel Halpern. New York: Henry Holt & Co., 1989.

Scenes from American Life: Contemporary Short Fiction. New York: Random House, 1973; New York: Vanguard, 1973.

Story: Fictions Past and Present. Edited by Joyce Carol Oates with Boyd Litzinger. Lexington, Mass.: Heath, 1985.

Uncollected Essays

"Art: Therapy and Magic." *American Journal* 1, no. 3 (3 July 1973): 17–20.

Afterword to *The Poisoned Kiss and Other Stories from the Portuguese.* Fernandes/ Joyce Carol Oates. New York: Vanguard, 1975, 187–89.

"Background and Foreground in Fiction." *Writer* 80 (August 1967): 11–13.

"Building Tension in the Short Story." *Writer* 79 (June 1966): 11–12, 44.

"Disguised Fiction." *PMLA* 89 (May 1974): 580–81.

"How is Fiction Doing?" *New York Times Book Review,* 14 December 1980, 5–6.

"An Imperative to Escape the Prison of Gender." *New York Times Book Review,* 15 April 1973, 7, 10, 12.

Introduction to *The Best American Short Stories 1979: Selected from US and Canadian Magazines.* Edited by Joyce Carol Oates with Shannon Ravenel. Boston: Houghton Mifflin, 1979, xi–xxii.

"Joyce Carol Oates on Thoreau's 'Walden.'" *Mademoiselle* 76 (April 1973), 96, 98.

"The Myth of the Isolated Artist." *Psychology Today* 6 (May 1973), 74–75.

"The Nature of Short Fiction; or, The Nature of My Short Fiction." In *Handbook of Short Story Writing,* edited by Frank A. Dickinson and Sandra Smythe. Cincinnati: Writer's Digest, 1970, xi–xviii.

"New Heaven and Earth." *Saturday Review* 55 (4 November 1972), 51–54.

"On Boxing." *New York Times Magazine,* 16 June 1985, 28–32, 34, 37–38.

"Out of the Machine." *Atlantic,* July 1971, 42–45.

"Other Celebrity Voices: How Art Has Touched Our Lives." *Today's Health* 52 (May 1974), 31.

"The Poet, the Self, and Nature," *Dialogue* 7, no. 1 (1974), 73–83.

Preface to *Critical Essays on Joyce Carol Oates,* edited by Linda W. Wagner. Boston: G. K. Hall, 1979, xi–xiii.

Preface to *Where Are You Going, Where Have You Been?: Stories of Young America.* Greenwich, Conn.: Fawcett, 1974, 8–10.

Remarks by Joyce Carol Oates upon accepting the 1970 National Book Award in Fiction for *them,* quoted in *December Magazine* 12, i–ii (1970), 215.

Review of *The Penguin Book of Women Poets. The New Republic* 21 (April 1979), 28–30.

Review of *The Simone Weil Reader,* edited by George A. Panichas. *New Republic* 177 (2 July 1977), 33–37. Reprinted in revised form, with personal passages deleted, in *The Profane Art.*

"Richard Wishnetsky: Joyce Carol Oates Supplies a Missing View." *Detroit Free Press,* 6 March 1966, 1–2, 12–13.

"The Short Story." *Southern Humanities Review* 5, no. 3 (Summer 1971), 213–14.

"A Special Message to the Members of the First Edition Society." In *Bellefleur* New York: Dutton, 1980.

"A Special Message to the Members of the First Edition Society." In *Mysteries of Winterthurn* New York: Dutton, 1984.

"Stories That Define Me: The Making of a Writer." *New York Times Book Review* 87 (11 July 1982), 1, 15–16.

"The Style of the 70's: The Novel." *New York Times Book Review* 82 (5 June 1977), 7, 40–41.

"A Terrible Beauty Is Born. How?" *New York Times Book Review* 90 (11 August 1985), 1, 27, 29.

"The Unique/Universal in Fiction." *Writer* 86 (January 1983), 9–12.

"Why Is Your Writing So Violent?" *New York Times Book Review* 86 (29 March 1981), 15, 35.

"Whose Side Are You On?" *New York Times Book Review* 77 (4 June 1972), 63.

SECONDARY WORKS

Bibliography

Lercangée, Francine. *Joyce Carol Oates: An Annotated Bibliography,* with a preface and annotations by Bruce F. Michelson. New York: Garland, 1986. "The first attempt to compile a comprehensive, partly annotated bibliography of the writings by and about Joyce Carol Oates." Covers works published from 1963 through August 1985; includes 1,937 listings. An invaluable source.

Interviews, Conversations, and Correspondence

A Moveable Feast. Interviews and readings on audiotape. Columbia, Mo.: American Audio Press Library, 1982. Oates reading from her work and discussing her craft.

Boesky, Dale. "Correspondence with Miss Joyce Carol Oates." *International Review of Psychoanalysis* 2 (1975): 481–86. Two very long letters in which Oates responds specifically and generally to questions about applied psychoanalysis and literature.

"Contemporary Authors Interview." In *Contemporary Authors,* edited by Hal May and Deborah A. Strait, new rev. ser., vol. 23. Detroit: Gale Research, 1989: 349–52. Oates's responses to questions about her writing habits, techniques, and recent works.

Kazin, Alfred. "Oates." *Harper's* (August 1971), 78–82. Essay based on interview, characterizing Oates as haunted and obsessed with a "sweetly brutal sense of what American experience is really like" and arguing that her fictionalizing of this experience is not always sufficiently shaped into art.

McCombs, Phil. "The Demonic Imagination of Joyce Carol Oates." *Washington Post*, 18 August 1986, C1, C11. Interview and article, with particular emphasis on personal background of *Marya: A Life*.

Milazzo, Lee, ed. *Conversations with Joyce Carol Oates*. Jackson: University Press of Mississippi, 1989. Collects major, previously published interviews and conversations from 1969 to 1989, which are not itemized separately in this bibliography. A very convenient collection of materials.

Pinsker, Sanford. "Speaking about Short Fiction: An Interview with Joyce Carol Oates." *Studies in Short Fiction* 18, no. 3 (Summer 1981), 239–43. Interview focusing on short stories.

Books

Bastian, Katherine. *Joyce Carol Oates's Short Stories Between Tradition and Innovation*. Frankfurt: Bern, Lang, 1983. Divides short stories into three subgenres: the extraordinary, recognition, and initiation. Demonstration of Oates's allegiances to and departures from literary tradition.

Bender, Eileen Teper. *Joyce Carol Oates, Artist in Residence*. Bloomington: Indiana University Press, 1987. Discussion of novels through 1986, stressing Oates's enrichment by the university community of discourse and by feminism.

Bloom, Harold, ed. *Modern Critical Views: Joyce Carol Oates*. New York: Chelsea House, 1987. Collection, in a series, of previously published material; with introduction.

Creighton, Joanne V. *Joyce Carol Oates*. Boston: Twayne, 1979. Comprehensive study of novels and short stories from 1963 to 1976, using Oates's essays and comments to help assess the implicit rhetoric of the texts.

Friedman, Ellen. *Joyce Carol Oates*. New York: Ungar, 1980. Reading of novels to 1978, stressing Oates's "inveterate antiromanticism" in her depiction of overreaching Faustian dreamers and the need to recognize human limitation and community.

Grant, Mary Kathryn. *The Tragic Vision of Joyce Carol Oates*. Durham, N.C.: Duke University Press, 1978. Examination of Oates's "tragically diminished characters" and the "hope of a hope" that the author will "find a shape for so much pain."

Johnson, Greg. *Understanding Joyce Carol Oates*. Columbia: University of South Carolina Press, 1987. Discussion of six novels and two short-story collections as a guide for students and nonacademic readers, stressing the unity of Oates's work and its exploration of American life and culture in the last half-century.

Norman, Torborg. *Isolation and Contact: A Study of Character Relationships in Joyce Carol Oates's Short Stories, 1963–1980*. Göteborg, Sweden: Acta Universitatis Gothoburgensis, 1984. Close reading of a number of Oates's short stories from the perspective of speech-act theory to explore how character and context are revealed through dialogue.

Wagner, Linda M., ed. *Critical Essays on Joyce Carol Oates.* Boston: G. K. Hall, 1979. Collection of 11 essays (most previously published and not listed separately in this bibliography), 17 reviews, an introduction by Wagner, and a preface by Oates, demonstrating a wide range of critical perspectives.

Waller, G. F. *Dreaming America: Obsession and Transcendence in the Fiction of Joyce Carol Oates.* Baton Rouge: Louisiana State University Press, 1979. Analysis of novels and critical essays, demonstrating the strong influence of D. H. Lawrence and stressing Oates's "neo-romantic" celebration of the flux of human experience and the possibility of transcending limitations.

Critical Essays

Allen, Mary I. "The Terrified Women of Joyce Carol Oates." In *The Necessary Blankness: Women in Major American Fiction of the Sixties.* Urbana: University of Illinois Press, 1976, 133–59. Finds Oates to be masterful at depicting women's blankness and pervasive terror of men, sexuality, motherhood, violence, lack of control.

Barza, Steven. "Joyce Carol Oates: Naturalism and the Aberrant Response." *Studies in American Fiction* 7 (1979), 141–51. Suggests that Oates's naturalistic fiction has a "stimulus-response dysfunction": a strong response with little or no stimulus.

Burwell, Rose Marie. "Joyce Carol Oates and an Old Master." *Critique: Essays in Modern Fiction* 15, no. 1 (1973), 48–58. Argues that Oates drew the title of *A Garden* from Hieronymous Bosch's sixteenth-century triptych and modeled the book's structure and imagery on those of the painting.

————. "The Process of Individuation as Narrative Structure: Joyce Carol Oates' *Do With Me What You Will.*" *Critique: Studies in Modern Fiction* 17, no. 2 (1975), 93–106. Analyzes the novel's structure and Elena's successful synthesizing of personality in terms of Jungian states of individuation.

————. "*Wonderland*: Paradigm of the Psychohistorical Mode." *Mosaic* 14, no. 3 (Summer 1981), 1–16. Treats the character Jesse, stressing historical and psychological contexts.

Chell, Cara. "Un-Tricking the Eye: Joyce Carol Oates and the Feminist Ghost Story." *Arizona Quarterly* 41, no. 1 (Spring 1985), 5–23. Finds a feminist subtext in *Mysteries of Winterthurn,* noting that the victim, Perdita, "metamorphosizes into the agent of her own wrath" and plots the final murders with Xavier.

Dean, Sharon L. "Faith and Art: Joyce Carol Oates's *Son of the Morning.*" *Critique: Essays on Modern Fiction* 28, no. 3 (Spring 1987), 135–47. Treats faith and its relationship to art in the novel.

Ditsky, John. "The Man on the Quaker Oates Box: Characteristics of Recent Experimental Fiction." *Georgia Review* 26 (Fall 1972), 297–313. Places Oates with experimentalists rather than realists "in spirit if not in form" because of her concern with "inner states" that are "the fragmented reflection . . . of the fragmented external world."

Giles, James R. "From Jimmy Gatz to Jules Wendall: A Study of 'Nothing Substantial.'" *Dalhousie Review* 56 (Winter 1976–77), 718–24. Parallels Jules from *them* with Gatsby, finding Oates's work to be a "respectful parody" of Fitzgerald's.

————. "'Suffering, Transcendence, and Artistic Form': Joyce Carol Oates's *them*." *Arizona Quarterly* 32 (Autumn 1976), 213–26. Argues that the tension between "naturalistic documentation of struggle and pain and romantic glorification of the human soul is critical to *them*": Loretta is destroyed, Maureen saved, and Jules transformed from an "idealistic rebel to a calculating nihilist."

————. "The 'Marivaudian Being' Drowns His Children: Dehumanization in Donald Barthelme's 'Robert Kennedy Saved from Drowning' and Joyce Carol Oates' *Wonderland*." *Southern Humanities Review* 9 (Winter 1975), 63–75. Argues that Barthelme's story and Oates's novel present two views of the "alienated and fragmented American of the sixties," who is equivalent to Poulet's "the Marivaudian being . . . a pastless futureless man, born anew at every moment."

Goodman, Charlotte. "Women and Madness in the Fiction of Joyce Carol Oates." *Women and Literature* 5, no. 2 (1977), 17–28. Claims that Oates "dramatizes forcefully some of the factors that contribute to the despair and psychological disintegration of contemporary women."

Harter, Carol. "America as 'Consumer Garden': The Nightmare Vision of Joyce Carol Oates." *Revue des Langues Vivantes,* bicentennial issue (1976), 171–87. Emphasizes the struggle of characters for liberation within the 'consumer garden' of American society in an overview of the novels from *A Garden* through *Wonderland*.

Karl, Frederick. *American Fictions, 1940–1980* (New York: Harper & Row, 1980), 298–302, 440–42, 546–49. Discusses *them,* Oates as a woman writer, and *Bellefleur*.

Keyser, Elizabeth Lennox. "*A Bloodsmoor Romance:* Joyce Carol Oates's Little Women." *Women's Studies* 14, no. 3 (1988), 211–23. Discusses parallels to Alcott's famous novel.

Madden, David. "The Violent World of Joyce Carol Oates." *The Poetic Image in 6 Genres.* Carbondale: Southern Illinois University Press, 1969, 26–46. Characterizes Oates as the "second finest writer in America" (after Wright Morris); she sustains the intensity of her vision and the credibility of her characters and situations despite aesthetic flaws and "an apparent absence of art."

Mickelson, Anne Z. "Sexual Love in the Fiction of Joyce Carol Oates." In *Reaching Out: Sensitivity and Order in Recent American Fiction by Women* (Metuchen, N.J.: Scarecrow Press, 1979), 15–34. Sees the oedipal conflict as a fundamental theme in Oates's fiction and criticizes the lack of "psychic development" in Oates's women characters.

Nodelman, Perry. "The Sense of Unending: Joyce Carol Oates's *Bellefleur* as Experiment in Feminine Storytelling." In *Breaking the Sequence: Women's Experimental Fiction,* edited by Ellen G. Friedman and Miriam Fuchs (Princeton, N.J.: Princeton University Press, 1989), 250–64. Argues that *Bellefleur's* narrative is a "denial of linear history" and, as such, "an identifiably feminine form of experimentation."

Pinsker, Sanford. "Joyce Carol Oates and the New Naturalism." *Southern Review* 15, no. 1 (Winter 1979), 52–63. Suggests that Oates has "affinities" with naturalism and with such contemporary writers as Heller and Pynchon.

Shepherd, Allen G., III. "Faulknerian Antecedents to Joyce Carol Oates's *Mysteries of Winterthurn.*" *Notes on Contemporary Literature* 17, no. 5 (November 1987), 8–10. Finds source for the novel in Faulkner's "A Rose for Emily."

Stout, Janis P. "Catatonia and Femininity in Oates's *Do With Me What You Will.*" *International Journal of Women's Studies* 6, no. 3 (May-June 1983), 208–15. Treats stereotypes of women and their relationship to passivity.

Taylor, Gordon O. "Joyce Carol Oates: Artist in Wonderland." *Southern Review* 10, no. 1 (1974), 490–503. Outlines the general structure of *Wonderland,* characterizing it as "inwardly spiraling, shell-like," and suggests that the whole body of Oates's work can be seen as a similar "impulsive intensification."

Wagner, Linda W. "Oates' *Cybele.*" *Notes on Contemporary Literature* 5, no. 2 (November 1981), 2–8. Notes parallels to the mythic Cybele and suggests that the character Edwin Locke is an ironic re-creation of John Locke.

Waller, G. F. "Joyce Carol Oates' *Wonderland:* An Introduction." *Dalhousie Review* 54 (Autumn 1974), 480–90. Finds *Wonderland* to be Oates's "most completely realized novel" and emphasizes its deterministic social context.

Wilson, Mary Ann. "From Thanatos to Eros: A Study of Erotic Love in Joyce Carol Oates' *Do With Me What You Will.*" *Studies in the Humanities* 11, no. 2 (December 1984), 48–55. Focuses on Oates's treatment of erotic love in the novel.

Index

The Author

Joanne V. Creighton, vice president for academic affairs and provost and professor of English at Wesleyan University, received her B.A. from the University of Wisconsin in 1964, her M.A. from Harvard University in 1965, and her Ph.D. from the University of Michigan in 1969. She taught English 17 years at Wayne State University, where she also served as associate dean of liberal arts and special assistant to the provost for humanities. At the University of North Carolina at Greensboro she served as dean of the College of Arts and Sciences and professor of English from 1985 to 1990. In addition to the earlier Twayne volume on Joyce Carol Oates (1979), Creighton is the author of *William Faulkner's Craft of Revision* (1977) and *Margaret Drabble* (1985).

The Editor

Warren French (Ph.D., University of Texas, Austin) retired from Indiana University in 1986 and is now an honorary professor associated with the Board of American Studies at the University College of Swansea, Wales. In 1985 Ohio University awarded him a doctor of humane letters. He has contributed volumes to Twayne's United States Authors Series on Jack Kerouac, Frank Norris, John Steinbeck, and J. D. Salinger. His most recent publication for Twayne is *The San Francisco Poetry Renaissance, 1955–1960.*